SAP FICO
BEGINNER'S HANDBOOK

Step by Step Screenshots Guided Handholding Approach to Learning

SAP for Dummies, SAP Books

Murugesan Ramaswamy

SAP FICO BEGINNER'S HANDBOOK (Ed-2.4)

http://sapficouser.com

Copyright © 2014 by Murugesan Ramaswamy

All rights reserved. No part of this publication may be reproduced, distributed or transmitted in any form or by any means, including photocopying, recording, or other electronic or mechanical methods, without the prior written permission of the publisher, except in the case of brief quotations embodied in critical reviews and certain other noncommercial uses permitted by copyright law.

SAP is the trademark of SAP AG Germany and we are not affiliated to them.

Author of this book has made every reasonable attempt to provide highest accuracy in the content of this book. However, he assumes no responsibility for errors or omissions. You should use this book as you deem fit and at your own risk. It is likely that the examples won't be applicable in your situation and you should adjust your use of the information and recommendation accordingly

Who can benefit from this book?

Explaining FI, CO modules & Concepts to guide **Consultants, Users, End Users and Super Users** gain confidence, get comfortable with and improve productivity using SAP FICO. Beginners who are in their First & Second year of career with SAP FICO will find this book beneficial the most.

HOW THE CHAPTERS ARE ARRANGED

Chapter I Helps YOU **begin using** SAP FICO on a strong note.

Chapter II Grasp the **concepts** for a theoretical foundation on which SAP FICO is designed and built.

Chapter III & IV Get introduced to **Transaction Codes & Standard Reports** in SAP FICO.

Chapter V Navigation in SAP FICO put YOU at **complete ease** with SAP Navigation and a strong footing to move forward **confidently**.

Chapter VI & VII Essential SAP Tips & Layout make YOUR SAP FICO experience **a pleasure**.

Chapter VIII Guide YOU to **work with Standard Reports**.

Chapter IX, X, XI Experience **authority** in using Standard Reports.

SAP VERSION

This book is based on SAP ECC 6 version.

ABOUT THE AUTHOR

Author of this book is a Chartered Accountant from India. He has over 25 years functional experience in Finance & Accounts. In SAP FICO domain he has participated from user side of SAP /ERP implementations in various roles such as Core Team Member, Project Manager and Process Owner.

Author of this book can be contacted at **murugesan0202@yahoo.com** or **admin@sapficouser.com**. For updates on new releases & subscribing to *SAP FICO USER News Letter* please visit http://sapficouser.com.

Table of Contents

Chapter I Navigation in SAP [Part-I] 1
   1. Login and Password Change 1
   2. SAP Screen Structure 3
   3. Command Window & Transaction Codes 4
   4. Stop Transaction 6
   5. Working with Multiple Sessions 7

Chapter II Concepts 9
   1. Enterprise Resource Planning 9
   2. Accounting Perspective of Data 11
   3. Chart of Accounts 14
   4. SAP as ERP 19
   5. Modules in SAP 20
   6. FICO - External and Internal Reporting 21
   7. Company Codes and Currencies 24
   8. Cost Centers 26
   9. Internal Orders 28
   10. Overhead Management with Cost Centers and Internal Orders 29
   11. Product Cost Planning 30
   12. Profit Center Accounting 30
   13. COPA - Profitability Analysis 31

Chapter III Data Entry 32

Chapter IV Standard Reports in FICO 36

Chapter V Navigation in SAP [Part-II] 38
   1. Menu Bar and Application Tool Bar, How they change with Different Applications 38
   2. Exporting report to Excel, Word, Mail 49
   3. Standard Tool Bar Icons 50

4.	Display TCodes in SAP Menu	53
5.	Status Bar for System Messages and Session Information	55
6.	Homework for you!	57

Chapter VI   SAP Tips & Tricks   58

1.	Favorites	58
2.	Desktop Shortcut for SAP Transaction	60
3.	Finding Transaction Code in SAP Menu	63
4.	Using Tab Options and Personal Value List in F4 help	65
5.	Copy Paste in SAP	68

Chapter VII   Customizing SAP Layout   70

1.	Quick Info	70
2.	Keys in Drop down List	72
3.	Changing the Font	73
4.	Automatic Tabbing at End of Field	75
5.	Cursor Behavior While Working in Lists	76

Chapter VIII   Report Parameter Selections   77

1.	Dynamic Selections, Where Used?	77
2.	Multiple Selection Icons	79
3.	Dynamic Selection icon	81
4.	Maintain Selection Options Icon and its Use	82
5.	Selection Variant	84
6.	Report Layout Changes	92
7.	Report Parameter by Default	96

Chapter IX   List Functions   99

1.	Sort Order - Simple & Multi Level	99
2.	Filter - Multi Level	102
3.	Subtotal - Simple and Multilevel	104
4.	Know what Filter, Sort, Subtotal criteria is applied to a List	107
5.	Display Variant	109

Chapter X   ABC Analysis   113
  1. Concept of ABC Analysis   113
  2. Key Figure Percentage Method   115
  3. Key Figure Absolute Method   117
  4. Attributes Percentage Method   118

Chapter XI   Extract Management   119

Chapter I Navigation in SAP [Part-I]

*Chapter to help YOU **begin using** SAP FICO on a strong note*

∞

Welcome to the fascinating world of SAP! This book attempts to help you crack the tricks of mastering SAP FICO. One-step at a time, no steps missed. You have the freedom to skip a topic if you find it you have already mastered it. However, I recommend reading the sub headings before you go to next topic. There is every possibility that there is a useful idea in that topic that is not known to you until now. End of the day I WANT YOU TO GET FULL BENEFIT of this book.

One word of caution though, reading this book will see that YOU HAVE BEGUN your journey of mastering SAP FICO. Learning is not a destination but a journey is very much true here.

Join me. Let us begin our Journey!

1. Login and Password Change

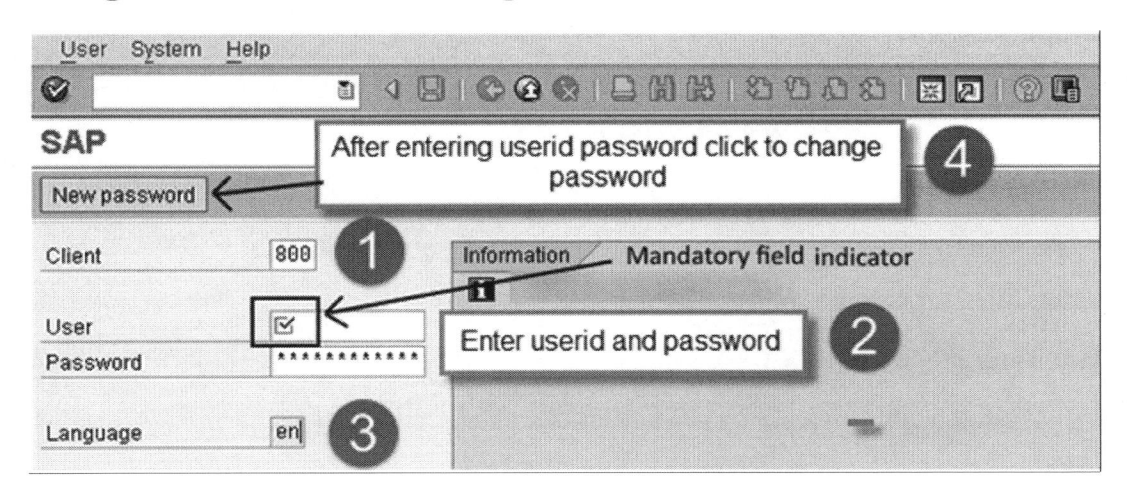

1. Client

Client is the 'Business Unit' that you will be using in SAP. You will not be prompted to make a selection here in a normal working environment. If at all you need to select take advice from your SAP System Admin team.

2. Login, User ID

System Admin Department will give you first time login user id & password. SAP system will prompt you to change the first time password.

3. Language

You can choose the language option. For English, the option is 'en'.

4. Password Change

For changing password (marked 4 in the picture), after entering your login id and password, click *'New Password'* icon, before pressing 'Enter' key. Note **Password Change option is available in the initial login screen**.

It is a good practice to change the password periodically.

Mandatory Field

Refer to the picture, whenever you see a small **tick mark** in a data entry field, it indicates that it is a mandatory field. You need to give a valid value for this field.

∞

2. SAP Screen Structure

Once you login SAP system you will go to 'SAP Easy Access' window. This window has the following structure:

1. Menu Bar
2. Command Window and Standard Tool Bar
3. Application Tool Bar
4. SAP Menu
5. Status Bar

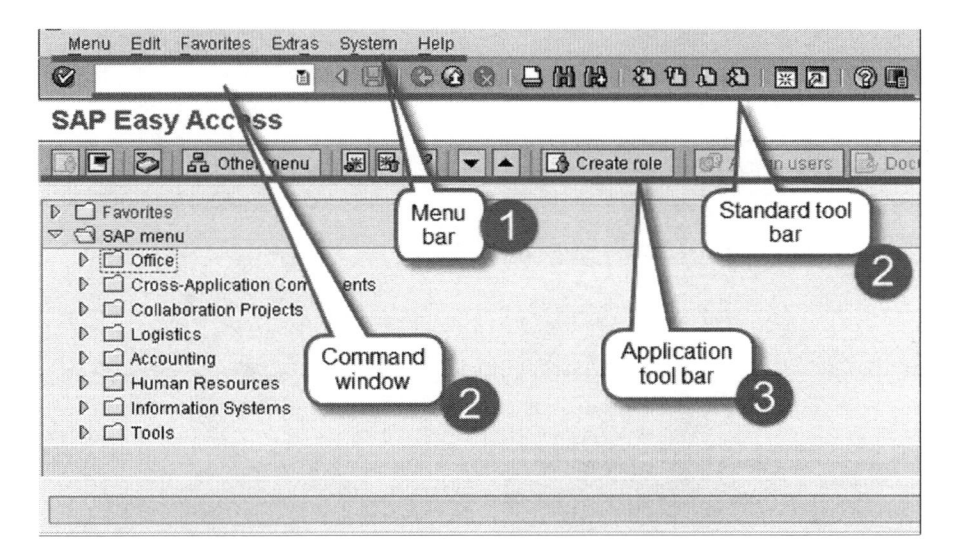

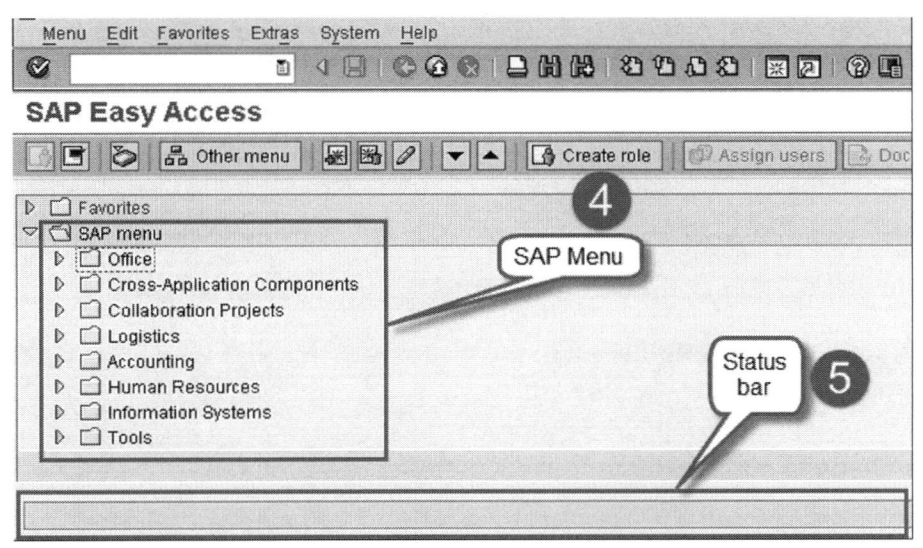

3. Command Window & Transaction Codes

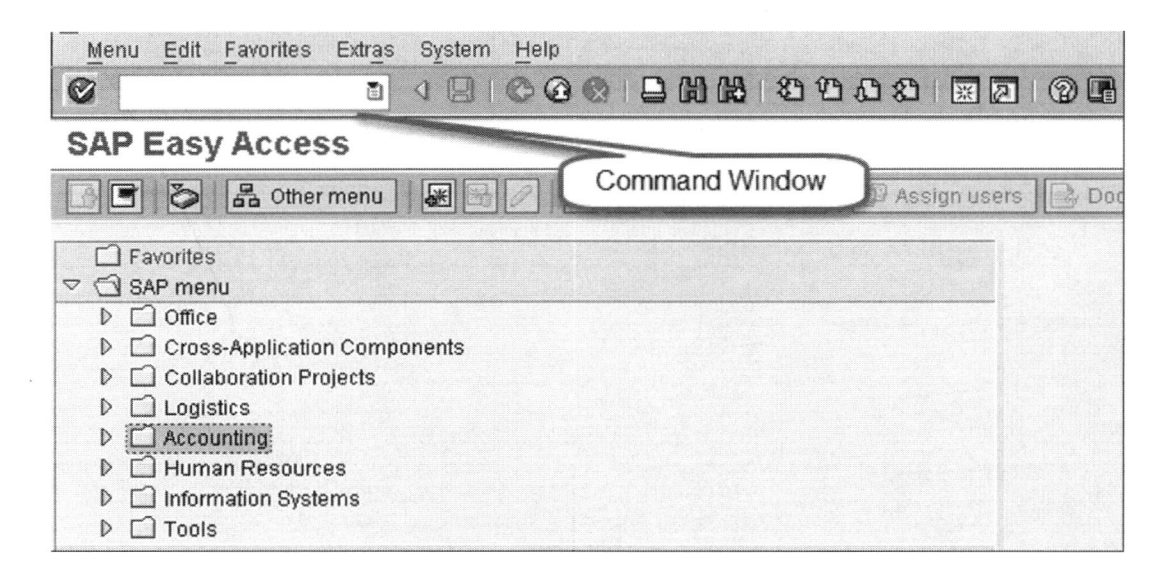

What is **Transaction Code or shortly TCode** and how it is used in SAP?

Whatever you need to achieve using the system it is done with a program. TCodes are the system names for the programs. TCodes come with suitable narrative descriptions to help you understand the purpose for which it is used.

Example of TCode: F-02 - General Posting, First part, 'F-02' is the TCode, Second part, 'General Posting' is the TCode description.

It is a good practice to memorize few of the often-used TCodes.

If you know the TCode for the program you want to run, you can enter it in the 'Command Window' and press 'Enter' key. System will take you to the screen of the TCode. This is one of the ways, by which you can improve SAP system navigation speed. We will see more useful tips along the way, how to save time in system navigation.

To open and close command window, click on the arrow to the right of the command window.

Previously used TCodes list

You can view the TCodes previously used in the 'command window' by clicking the 'pointer' on the right side within the command window. This has an obvious advantage, you can select a TCode in the drop down list and press 'Enter' to quickly run the program.

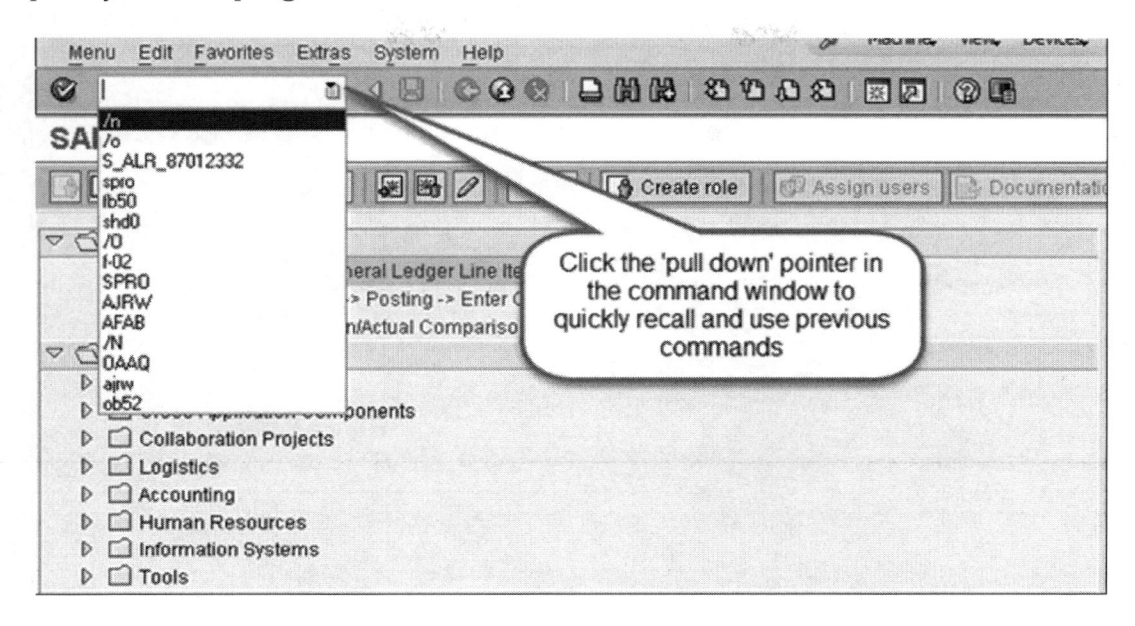

Using '/n'

Say, you are in a List display screen. Now you want to quit this screen and go to a transaction screen FB50.

Type '**/nfb50**' in the Command Window and press 'Enter'. System takes you to the 'fb50' screen.

Using '/o'

Say, you want to open transaction fb50 in a new session. (Refer Page 7).

Type '**/ofb50**' in the Command Window and press 'Enter'. System takes you to fb50 transaction in a new session.

4. Stop Transaction

Consider a situation when you have started a transaction in the system accidentally and the system takes long time to process this transaction.

Under the above circumstance you can 'stop transaction' using menu option.

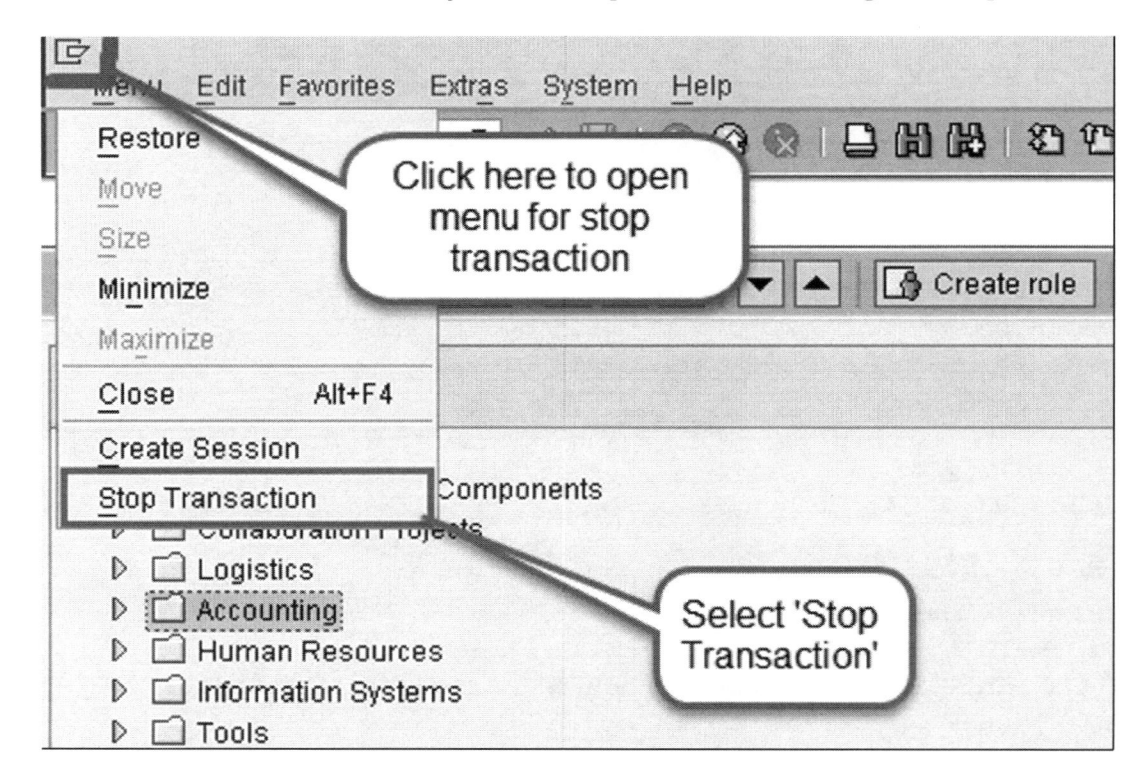

Open the menu by clicking the small pointer at the top left corner of the screen. Choose 'Stop Transaction' to terminate the transaction.

5. Working with Multiple Sessions

Menu path: System >> Create Session

Application Tool Bar: [icon] New Session icon

A session is an open SAP window. You may open up to **6 sessions** and work on a system task in each session. It is always a good idea to have two sessions open.

Left-click on the 'New Session' button to create a new session.

There is yet another way to start a new session using the context menu. Select your transaction in SAP Menu, right click and choose 'Execute in new window'.

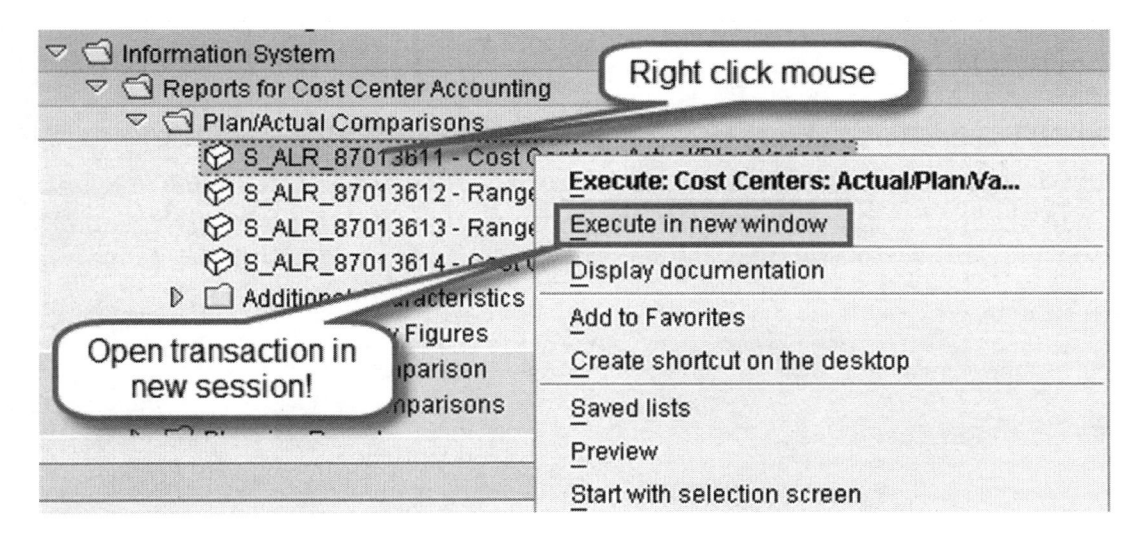

Logoff multiple sessions in one step

Your boss is waiting for you in the conference room in the midst of a meeting. You have many SAP sessions open and you do not want the SAP system open, when you are away.

Choose menu path 'System >> Log off'. System prompts 'Unsaved data will be lost, do you want to Log off?'. Click 'Yes'. You are 'logged off' all the sessions in one go.

Take care in case if you are in the midst of a data entry you run the risk of losing unsaved data!

8 SAP FICO BEGINNER'S HANDBOOK

We will cover the following topics in Navigation in SAP Part - II:

1. Menu Bar and Application Tool Bar in:
   - SAP Easy Access Screen
   - Data Entry Screen
   - Selection Screen
   - List Screen
   - Report Screen
2. Exporting report to Excel, Word, Mail
3. Standard Tool Bar Icons explained
4. Display TCodes in SAP Menu
5. Status Bar for system messages and Session information display
6. Home work for you!

To continue reading on Navigation in SAP, please go to Page 38.

Even if you choose to skip the next chapters and go to Navigation in SAP - Part II now, I suggest you read Chapters on Concepts, Data Entry & Standard Reports (Chapters II, III,& IV) later to gain essntial insigt on theoritical basis behind SAP FICO.

∞∞

Chapter II Concepts

Sometimes a concept is baffling not because it is profound but because it is wrong. **E. O. Wilson**

Grasp the concepts for a theoretical foundation on which SAP FICO is designed and built

∞

1. Enterprise Resource Planning

ERP stands for Enterprise Resource Planning. ERP is an Information System designed to collect, process and report on Financial & Non Financial information of an Organization with a view to Plan, Direct and Control its performance.

Essential characteristics of an ERP

> Data Capture at the point of action. In other words, data is fed in to respective system components called Modules where the real time transaction takes place

> Sharing of information, both Transaction Data and Master Data between Modules of the System (Refer to Page 11 for a discussion on Transaction and Master data).

ERP system enables:

- Data Collection
- Data Processing
- Providing Information in the form of Reports

ERP enhances an Organizations capability in Planning, Monitoring Progress and Exercise Control, Reduce Wastage and Inefficient Operations, Analyze Results to take corrective action where required.

ERP helps steering an organization towards achieving its Mission and Vision.

Let us briefly touch upon how ERP evolved:

- 1960s Inventory Control Packages
- 1970s MRP I Material Requirements Planning
- 1980s MRP II Manufacture Resources Planning
- 1990s Enterprise Resource Planning

∞

2. Accounting Perspective of Data

Let us understand basic terms used in Financial Accounting and Internal Management Reporting.

Master Data

Master data is the data that remains **constant over a period of time**. Examples are Customers and Suppliers name and contact details. In Materials Management name and specifications of materials are master data. In General Ledger, Account codes are master data.

Transaction Data

Activities of an organization, say sales, purchases, expenses etc., are recorded in the system. These entries in the system constitute transaction data. Every transaction data is linked to one or more master data. Example - Sales transactions linked with Customer Master Data. Transaction data are associated with a **specific period in time**, say sales on 15th Mar 2014.

Line Items & Statement of Account

Every transaction recorded in the system has two line items. One for debit and another for credit. When you want to study the transactions recorded under a GL account for a given period you run statement of account report for that account. The statement of account is the listing of line items.

Period Closing

In accounting perspective period is usually a calendar month. Period closing is a procedure of freezing data entry for a period. Period closing is done in the system, before analyzing the transaction data pertaining to a period. In order to convert the data for a period into useful information much elaborate procedure is followed as part of period closing. Simple examples could be depreciation of fixed assets calculation and posting them in the respective GL accounts, making provisions for expenses incurred and yet to be paid such as utility bills etc. In real time scenario and in systems like SAP it is a dedicated procedure involving multiple system components and departments.

Data Integrity

Data integrity is data reliability; different reports run correlate and not contradict with each other. E.g supplier control account balance as extracted from GL report should always match with grand total of individual suppliers' accounts as extracted from Supplier Sub Ledger.

To ensure data integrity, system design should enable data capture only once in the system. Example can be when sales are recorded in 'Sales and Distribution' component of a system, the same sales should not be entered in GL Sales account. Instead, the SD component should populate necessary sales transaction data to GL accounts. The process by which data from SD component is populated in GL accounts of FI is known as **integration** in system parlance.

Posting, Posted and Un-posted Transactions

Posting a transaction takes the data to the database, storing them in tables. Once a transaction is posted, it is available in reports. Usually systems provide for two stages of transaction entry. First stage, un-posted (SAP parlance - **Parked**) and the second stage posted. When the transaction that is being captured need to be verified it is kept in un-posted mode. It is 'posted' after verification. Once posted it cannot be changed to un-posted mode. If the posted data is found to be incorrect, it can be corrected through another entry, say a correction or reversal entry depending on system design.

Once period closing is completed, no further transactions postings are allowed in that period. Any correction required can be done only in the next open period.

Reconciliation

It is a process of establishing the relationship between two different data sources. Good example is bank reconciliation, balance as per company is related to balance as shown in bank statement. In a non-integrated system environment, this task will be a huge one. An ERP system ensures an integrated environment and thus requirement for reconciliation is to the minimum.

Integration

In system parlance, automated and secured connectivity of two otherwise independent components of a system makes an Integrated System. SAP is an integrated system. Integration enables transaction and master data captured in one component available in other components where and when required. Integration enables and facilitates data flow between system components. Example is customer master data entered in 'Sales and Distribution' module, is available in 'Financial Accounting' module; purchase transaction captured in 'Materials Management' module flows to 'Financial Accounting'. Fully integrated components make an ERP system.

Recurring Journal Voucher

This can be explained well through an example - you have to make entry, debit rent and credit rent payable, every month. There is no change in GL Account codes and amount. Here you can define recurring JV in the system with a 'from' and 'to' dates, say for one year. Any number of such entries can be grouped and defined as recurring JVs. You need to run a recurring JV program beginning of a month, system passes all the entries for you.

Reversal JV

Let us see an example here again, some organizations want to charge interest for the amount used in the business, though no money is borrowed from outside parties. This is called imputed interest. In such a scenario, you can use 'Reversal JV'. Entry to debit interest, credit imputed interest is passed in one period. Beginning of next period the entry is reversed. Through reversal entry functionality, this can be automated in the system.

JV Templates

You are required to record say, utility bills every month, end of first week of the period. Here essentially the debits and credits flow to the same respective GL Accounts. Only the amount varies from month to month. In this scenario, you can use JV template. During data entry, use the previously defined template in the system to insert only the amounts and post. This saves time in data entry.

3. Chart of Accounts

Balance Sheet Account Codes

Account Group	GL Code	GL Description
Current Assets	1001	Cash in Hand
	1003	Cash at Bank
	1005	Inventory
	1008	Accounts Receivable
	1012	Prepaid Expense
	1015	Short Term Deposits
Long Term Assets	1200	Land
	1300	Buildings
	1301	Accumulated Depreciation, Buildings
	1400	Vehicles
	1401	Accumulated Depreciation, Vehicles
	1600	Plant and Machinery
	1601	Accumulated Depreciation, Plant and Machinery
	1700	Office Equipment
	1701	Accumulated Depreciation, Office Equipment
	1800	Long Term Deposits
Current Liabilities	2002	Accounts Payable
	2100	Employment Tax Payable
	2300	Short Term Borrowings
	2350	Customer Deposits
	2385	Current Portion of Long Term Debt
	2400	Accrued Expenses
Capital & Long Term Liabilities	2505	Shareholders Equity
	2510	Profit and Loss Account
	2515	Long Term Borrowings

Control Account: Customer Sub-ledger entries flow here, no direct posting allowed (1008 Accounts Receivable)

ERP Environment: Postings from Assets Component, no direct posting allowed (1300–1701)

Control Account: Payable Sub-ledger entries flow here, no direct posting allowed (2002 Accounts Payable)

Profit & Loss Account Codes

Account Group	GL Code	GL Description
Income Accounts	3010	Sales
	3015	Other income
Direct Expense Accounts	4010	Materials
	4015	Freight
	4016	Direct Wages
	4023	Rental Expense
	4027	Repair and Maintenance
Indirect Expense Accounts (Overhead)	5010	Salaries & Benefits
	5015	Office Rental
	5312	Repair and Maintenance, Office
	5330	Postage
	5341	Telephone
	5345	Utilities
	5355	Office Supplies
	5358	Dues and Subscriptions
	5550	Insurance
	5600	Training
	5618	Taxes and Licenses
	5700	Legal Fees
	5762	Advertising
	5775	Research and Development
	5813	Depreciation Expense
	5820	Bank Fees
Other Accounts	7050	Interest Income
	7100	Cash Discounts
	7200	Gain or Loss on Sale of Assets

Chart of Accounts is the backbone and foundation for Accounting information classification (Accounting) and presentation (Reporting).

GL Account Groups and Sub Groups

General Ledger (GL) Accounts in Financial Accounting form the bricks for building the CoA superstructure. As you build living room, dining hall, kitchen and bedroom for your home you need GL Accounts in to a grouping structure. In other words, GL Account Groups and Sub Groups form the Chart of Accounts structure.

CoA Group Structure is decided based on statutory reporting requirements.

GL Account Groups for Balance Sheet

- Fixed Assets,
- Current Assets
- Current Liabilities
- Long Term Liabilities

GL Account Groups for Profit and Loss account

- Income Accounts
- Direct Expenses
- Overheads

This is only narrative, you will find more groupings in practice.

Sub Groups are sub classifications under the given Group. Example of Sub Groups under Balance Sheet - Current Assets main group:

- Stock
- Debtors
- Loans and Advances
- Cash and Bank

Here we say two levels of Grouping, main group and sub-group. You will see more levels depending on the size of the organization and complexity of the business.

Groups and Sub Groups come in handy to generate summarized financial reports- Balance Sheet and Profit and Loss Account. Summarized financial reports with comparative figures say, Current Year and Previous Year will enable the user of the report to quickly see major deviations. For example, you are interested in knowing the two years Current Assets, a Balance Sheet report generated with First Level GL Account Groups helps.

Summarized Financial Reports save time to further focus only on exceptions.

Sub-Ledger and Control Account

An organization transacts business with outsiders also known as business partners for purchasing of goods and services, sales and so on. So it becomes necessary to keep a record of say all the purchases and payments with a party in an Account. All such party accounts are grouped as Vendors and is recorded separately as Vendor Sub Ledger. A Sub Ledger is a separate component of a computerized Accounting system. Here we need to link the Vendor Sub Ledger to GL. A special Account called Control Account is defined in GL. Yes, Control Account is the linking pin between all the Vendors in Sub Ledger and the GL!

So what is unique about a Control Account? No direct postings allowed! System posts an entry as and when a purchase, payment or other adjustments is recorded in one of the Vendor Account in the Sub Ledger. You will now know that the net total of all the Vendor Sub Ledger Accounts should exactly match with the related GL Control Account.

Like Vendors Sub Ledger, there is a Sub Ledger for Customers and a corresponding GL Control Account in the Chart of Account.

GL Account Codes and Description

Every GL Account has two parts, Code and Description. Code is used by the computer system to identify the GL Account and is unique. Codes can be numerical and alphanumerical. Numerical codes are used by most systems. These codes have predefined number of digits.

Description is for the reader to infer what the GL Account stands for.

An example can be 600410 Printing and Stationery.

ERP Environment

An ERP environment is characterized by information capture and record at the origin of the transaction event. For example, Sales is recorded in Sales and Distribution (SD) Component of the ERP system by Sales Department of the organization. SD component is designed to provide complete support for all related functions of Marketing, Sales and Distribution.

Sales Account in GL in an ERP environment is designed with Control Account Properties, accepting entries only from Sales and Distribution Component.

You will find more GL Accounts act like a Control Account that accepts entries only from the related systems such as Asset Accounting, Personnel Accounting and Materials Management.

SAP and Chart of Accounts

By design, SAP differentiates between external statutory reporting and internal management reporting. The CoA is designed in Financial Accounting module to serve external reporting requirements. Internal management reporting is handled in 'Controlling' module via 'Primary Cost Elements', which are in many respects like GL Accounts. We will see more about internal and external reporting in a later section.

∞

4. SAP as ERP

In the business context, SAP is an *Information Technology System* designed module-wise. SAP Modules are designed around departments like Finance, Management Reporting, Human Resources, Material Management, Sales & Distribution and so on.

Departments are not stand-alone units, but highly interactive, interconnected sub entities of larger Business entity. Examples -Material Management interacts with Finance for Vendor payment, with Production for Issue of Raw materials, Receipt of Finished goods.

Accordingly, SAP Modules designed for the departments are capable of interacting with other modules, better known as *Integration*. Thus, there is integration between Finance & Management Information System, Finance & Materials Management, Finance & Human Resources and so on. In other words, **integration means flow of Transaction Data and sharing of Master Data** between Modules.

SAP R3 System

SAP is often referred to as R3 system. R3 stands for 3-tier architecture of SAP:

1. Database Layer, the database managed with DBMS in a server environment
2. Application Layer
3. Presentation Layer, the Graphical User Interface - GUI

Continue reading to know more on how SAP modules are designed.

∞

5. Modules in SAP

In the previous section, we had an introduction about SAP. Let us see how modules in SAP are designed.

SAP as an Information System is designed to capture Business Functions. So, Modules are built around Business Functions, often referred and understood as Departments.

Business Functions or Departments

Purchasing + Human Resources Management + Plant Maintenance >> Production + Inventory Management >> Sales and Distribution

Support Business Functions

Financial Accounting + Internal Management Reporting

Business Functions and SAP Modules

- Financial Accounting >> ***Financial Accounting - FI***
- Internal Management Reporting >> ***Controlling - CO***
- Purchasing & Inventory Management >> ***Materials Management - MM***
- Plant Maintenance >> ***Plant Maintenance***
- Production >> ***Production, Production Process***
- Human Resources >> ***Human Resources -- HR***
- Sales & Distribution >> ***Sales and Distribution - SD***

IMPORTANT: Above list is NOT meant to be an exhaustive list.

Let us know more about Financial Accounting and Controlling modules, often referred together as FICO in the following section.

6. FICO - External and Internal Reporting

We had an introduction to SAP Modules in the previous section. Let us understand more about FICO modules now.

External Reporting and Internal Reporting

Accounting seeks to record, classify and present business transactions that satisfy

- External reporting such as Government
- Internal reporting for management decision making

Financial Accounting (FI) is for *external financial reporting* and **Controlling (CO) is for** *internal management reporting*.

Data Capture in Financial Accounting

Organizations' transactions are captured in Financial Accounting through 1) Direct data entry and 2) Data flow, also known as integration from other modules - Asset Accounting, Materials Management, Payroll Accounting and Sales and Distribution. In the FI module, the data so collected is helpful in fulfilling the external legal reporting requirements.

Data Flow to Controlling using Primary Cost Elements

All expense and revenue data for the CO, the Internal Management Reporting module flows from FI module *seamlessly.* This seamless data flow from FI to CO is achieved through **Primary Cost Elements**. Primary Cost Elements and GL account codes are related on **one to one** relationship. By design, every expense and revenue GL account there is one Cost Element. GL account description is the default description for primary cost element. Remember GL account is for FI module and Cost Element is for CO module.

Company Codes and Currencies

Company Codes represent the legal status of an organization. Also Companies are required to make their legal reporting in a particular currency. Thus Company Codes and Currencies are defined and used in FI module for the data capture. We will see more about Company Codes and Currencies in a later section.

Controlling Area

Controlling Area is the organization unit in CO module. Controlling Area occupies the top node in CO under which Cost Centers and Internal Orders are defined and used in the cost management and cost monitoring.

We will see more about Cost Centers and Internal Orders under the respective sections.

Key Components of CO

Controlling module components include

- Overhead Cost Management consisting of Cost Centers and Internal Orders
- Product Cost Planning
- Profitability Analysis
- Profit Center Accounting

We will see more on these CO components in the coming sections.

SAP Cost Elements- Primary & Secondary

Cost and Revenue Elements are divided into

1. Primary Cost Elements for cost flows from Financial Accounting to Controlling
2. Secondary Cost Elements for cost flows within Controlling

Primary Cost Element Groups

We have seen GL account groups in Chart of Account. Similarly, Primary Cost Elements grouping is required in 'Controlling' module. While grouping Cost Elements, <u>internal reporting requirements</u> should be the consideration. So Cost Element Groups can be

- Personnel Costs
- Service & Operating Supplies
- Total Maintenance Costs
- Miscellaneous Overhead Costs

Depending on the nature of business, grouping can vary. In addition, one primary cost element may be present in more than one group. Example 'Salaries' cost element included in 'Total costs' and 'Personal Costs' groups.

Cost Element groups are useful in

- Reports, say Service & Operating Supplies costs reports
- Collective processing, say Planning for Total Maintenance Costs

7. Company Codes and Currencies

Company Codes and Currencies are defined and used in Financial Accounting - FI module.

Company Codes

Company Code defines the Legal Status of an organization. All external, legal reporting is based on Company Codes. There can be more than one Company Codes in an organization. Same way SAP system may be designed to capture information relating to multiple Company Codes. While data is entered in a system, correct Company Code should be given.

It derives to another point: Cross Company Code transactions. Say for example material belonging to Company A may be taken and used in a production process by Company B. Please note both Company A and B belong to same business organization. This involves Cross Company Code transactions. Capturing all this information is possible in SAP.

Currencies

Every financial information should be recorded with the correct Currency. Multiple currencies should be defined in the system.

One currency will be **Company Code currency**. As a Company is a legal entity, the Company Report should be made in a currency of the place where the Company is registered. This currency is Company Code Currency or **Reporting Currency** and is defined as such in the SAP system.

For organization having operations over more than one country, usually will have multiple reporting currencies.

Now to draw report at the Organization level, one currency is required. It is **Group Currency** and is defined in the system as such.

There may be transactions that happen in a currency other than a Company Code currency. Example a Company registered in US, with USD as Company Code currency buying goods from UK in GBP. Now in this case GBP is **Transaction Currency**.

Therefore, there are three types of currencies, Company Code or Reporting Currency, Group Currency and Transaction Currency. System should have means to translate between these currencies. This is achieved through defining Exchange Rates in the system.

∞

8. Cost Centers

Cost Centers are defined and used in Controlling - CO module under Controlling Area.

Menu path: SAP Menu >> Accounting >> Controlling >> Cost Center Accounting

Business Organizations *incur costs*, thus creating *value addition* to produce products or services or both.

Types of Costs

Costs are of two types

- Direct costs, Direct Material & Direct Labor
- Overheads - all the remaining costs

Controlling overheads is often a challenge. Cost Center is one of the tools designed to plan and control the overheads.

Overheads Classification

Overheads are classified under the headings -

- Manufacturing
- Marketing
- Selling and Distribution
- Administrative

This overhead cost classification is the first level in the pursuit of planning and control the costs.

Cost Centers

Next level is identify and define Cost Centers (CC). Thus Cost Centers are identifiable segment of an organization where in overheads are incurred, recorded, classified, planned and controlled.

Cost Centers may be identified and defined by

- Departments, say Purchase Department, Sales Department, Stores, Accounts, Maintenance, Quality Control, Human Resources and IT Department
- Set of Machines or a single large machinery

Cost Center, thus aids in collection of overheads in a meaningful and understandable way.

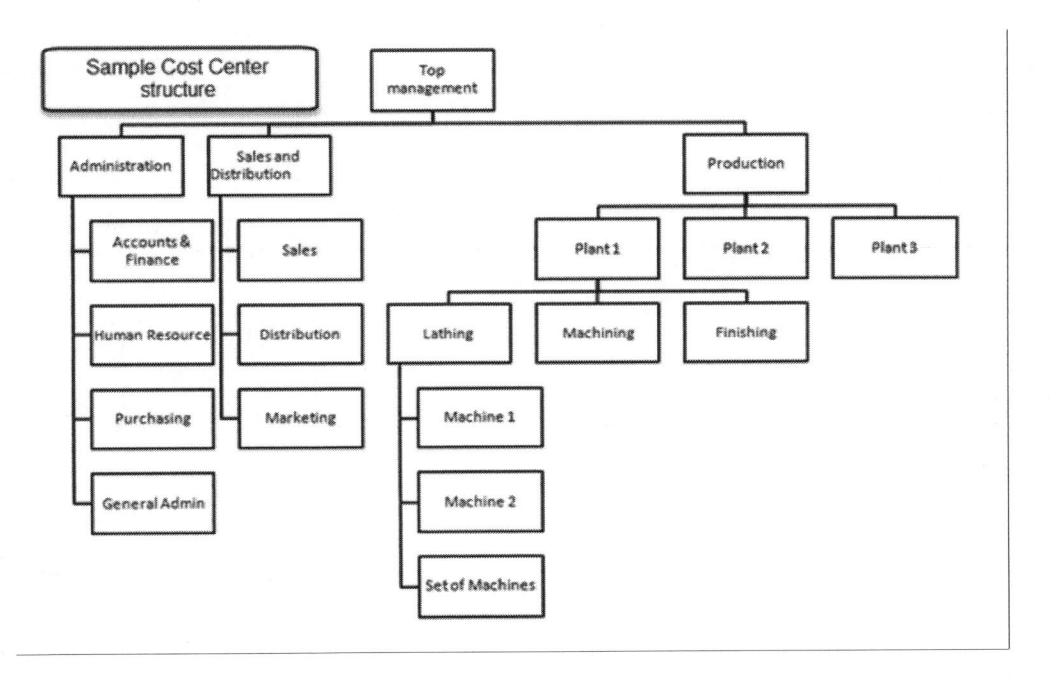

[Diagram: Sample Cost Center structure showing Top management with branches Administration (Accounts & Finance, Human Resource, Purchasing, General Admin), Sales and Distribution (Sales, Distribution, Marketing), and Production (Plant 1, Plant 2, Plant 3); Plant 1 contains Lathing, Machining, Finishing; Lathing contains Machine 1, Machine 2, Set of Machines]

Planning and Control of Overheads

Towards achieving the objective of planning and control of overheads, every Cost Center should be assigned with a manager as 'Person Responsible'. By making a person in charge of each Cost Center it is possible to make them accountable and responsible for the respective Cost Center expenses. Hence, cost control becomes manageable.

Person responsible for the Cost Centers will

- Have access to Cost Center reports
- Participate in planning costs
    - Have good understanding of cost flows between Cost Centers

9. Internal Orders

Menu path: SAP Menu >> Accounting >> Controlling >> Internal Orders

Different kinds of Internal Orders

Short-term event cost monitoring - events like Corporate Training to staff, Advertisement Campaign, Conducting Seminar, where cost may flow from more than one cost center or benefit may accrue to more than one cost center. Example -benefit of staff training where in staff from more than one department participate.

Internal Order may be designed to **monitor cost and revenue** of non-core business activities such as rent income from warehouses let out by an entity whose core business is manufacturing.

Internal Orders are used in Overhead Management as **Overhead Orders**.

Internal Orders are used for **Investment Purpose**, during construction of an asset, to collect all related expenses, later to be passed on to the Asset account.

Internal Orders as Accrual Cost collectors, example Annual Bonus payable to staff may be computed month on month and collected in an Internal Order. This is useful for the period based performance analysis such as monthly management reports. Thus, not only the incurred costs such as salary but also the accrued cost like bonus payable end of the fiscal year is considered to measure performance for a period.

Internal Orders as Production Orders or Process Orders and Sales Orders are used to track cost of a production batch or production of a unit, or a Sales Order.

Statistical Internal Orders are used for cost analysis purpose. No further cost flow happens from internal orders of this kind. Technically entries to these orders are called statistical posting.

SAP provides tools to manage internal orders such as allowing or not allowing entries to it, how the cost from the order will flow, budget control and so on, thus helping an organization to monitor, analyze and control cost.

10. Overhead Management with Cost Centers and Internal Orders

Cost Centers and Internal Orders complement each other in Overhead Cost Management.

Cost Centers are more of a permanent nature. They are designed for cost collecting and cost sending missions. Cost Centers are designed around departments/ functions under a manager who will hold responsibility for cost control of that department or function. Once the costs are collected, it is sent to Receiving Cost Centers or Internal Orders. Departments or functions serve other departments/ functions or to products produced. Hence, the cost has to flow to other departments/ functions / products. In the case of products, costs flow to Production Orders or Process Orders, which are one form of Internal Orders.

Internal Orders are more of short-term nature. Thus when a Production of a batch is completed the respective Production Order is Closed. For a closed internal order, postings are not permitted. However, analysis of costs recorded in the closed orders is possible.

The costs that flow to the Internal Orders are settled to the value of products, that may be semi finished or finished or passed on to Profitability Analysis (COPA) (Page 31) as in the case of Administrative Overhead and Sales and Distribution Overhead.

Thus, Cost Centers and Internal Orders complement each other in the Overhead Cost Management.

Important: It should not be construed as Internal Orders are used only for Overhead Cost Management. Please refer to section 'Internal Orders' Page 28 .

∞

11. Product Cost Planning

Product Cost Planning handles determination of standard cost of products manufactured by the company supporting key business decisions such as determining floor price of the products and calculation & analysis of variance.

12. Profit Center Accounting

Profit Centers are Responsibility Centers, Profit Center Accounting is also known as Responsibility Accounting.

Profit Centers are defined around products or product lines, geographical locations and in some cases around departments like production.

Profit Center Accounting helps delegation of authority and responsibility by making managers accountable for profit center performance.

SAP system helps measure Profit or Loss of individual profit centers. System supports Profit Center-wise pricing for goods transferred between them by a concept known as **Parallel Value Flows /Transfer Prices** without affecting company performance measure of Profit & Loss.

Technically, Profit Center accounting is a statistical accounting. No true postings happen in Profit Center accounting.

During data entry, profit center is not given explicitly, but the system is designed to derive the Profit Center.

∞

13. COPA - Profitability Analysis

Menu path: Accounting >> Controlling >> Profitability Analysis

Profitability Analysis is a component of SAP 'Controlling' module. COPA is designed to measure market segment-wise performance. The market segments can be based on customers, products or regions and so on.

Performance related data - cost & related revenue flows to COPA from

1. **Cost data** from Cost Centers, Internal Orders of Controlling
2. **Direct Posting** entries from General Ledger - FI
3. **Sales data** - sales revenue & sales quantity from SD
4. Any relevant data from **external systems**

COPA classifies the data in terms of Profitability Segments. **Profitability Segments are designed around market segments** in which the organization operates. Thus, COPA helps to analyze how the different market segments perform in terms of

- Profit & Loss
- Further cost break down into cost of goods sold, overheads and variances

∞∞

Chapter III   Data Entry

*Get introduced to **Transaction Codes** in SAP FICO*

∞

<u>DATA CAPTURE in SAP FI</u> happens through

1. DATA FLOW from Other Modules:

   - Sales data from SD
   - Payroll data from HR
   - Purchase data from MM

2. DATA ENTRY for

   - Events that happen in Finance & Accounts Department; example: Payment to a Vendor, Payment from a Customer, Purchases of office equipment, Petty cash expenses and so on.
   - Period Closing / Adjustment / Correction entries.

Transaction data from other modules flow to FI through **Integration**.

<u>DATA for CO module</u> flows from FI seamlessly, through Primary Cost Elements.

Data Entry in FI

During data entry in FI, you will have to choose one FI component and one CO component. For FI it is General Ledger Account code. For CO it is Cost Center or Internal Order.

Though data from FI flows to CO through Primary Cost Elements, choosing Cost Center or Internal Order during data entry is necessary to facilitate cost analysis in CO.

Example, Salaries to be accounted in GL account -Salaries, CO primary cost element -Salaries and cost center, say Admin. When you choose GL account code, primary cost element is automatically determined by system. You need to choose the cost center, Admin.

Understanding SAP Menu Hierarchy Logic helps grasp the SAP system easier. Let us look at some FICO relevant **Data Entry Menu, Transaction Codes and Description**. Again, this is NOT meant to be an exhaustive list.

General Ledger

Menu path: Accounting >> Financial Accounting >> General Ledger

i) General Ledger >> Posting

- F-02 Journal Voucher recording
- FB50 Enter GL Account Document

ii) General Ledger >> Document

- FB03 Display of Journal Voucher

iii General Ledger >> Document >> Reverse

- FB08 Reversal

Accounts Payable

Menu path: Accounting >> Financial Accounting >> Accounts Payable

i) Accounts Payable >> Document Entry

- FB60, F-43 Vendor Invoice Posting
- FB65, F-41 Vendor Credit Memo Posting

ii) Accounts Payable >> Document Entry >> Outgoing Payment

- F-53, F-58 Vendor Invoice Payment

iii Accounts Payable >> Document Entry >> Down Payment

- F-48, Advance Payment to Vendor
- F-54 Clearing the Down Payment

Accounts Receivable

Menu path: Accounting >> Financial Accounting >> Accounts Receivable

i) Accounts Receivable >> Document Entry

- FB70, F-22 Invoice
- F-28 Incoming Payments

ii) Accounts Receivable >> Document Entry >> Down Payment

- F-29 Customer Advance
- F-39 Clearing Advance

iii) Accounts Receivable >> Document Entry >> Other

- F-31, F-18 Refund of Customer Advance

iv) Accounts Receivable >> Account

- F-32 Clear Customer Invoice with Advance

Bank and Cash Transaction

Menu path: Accounting >> Financial Accounting

i) Financial Accounting >> Banks >> Environment >> Check Balance >> Display

- FCHN Display Checks Register

ii) Financial Accounting >> Accounts Payable >> Documents >> More Functions

- FBZ5 Printing Checks

Asset Accounting

AS01 Creation of Asset Master

AS11 Creation of Asset Sub number

AW01N Asset Explorer, to display all asset data including acquisition, planned depreciation, posted depreciation, useful life.

Logistics

Menu path: Logistics >> Logistics Execution >> Transportation >> Shipment Costs >> Freight Invoice Check >> Logistics Invoice Verification >> Document Entry

- MIRO Enter Invoice

Menu path: Logistics >> Logistics Execution >> Inbound Process >> Goods Receipt for Purchase Order, Order, Other Transactions

- MIGO - Enter Goods Receipt for Purchase Order

∞∞

Chapter IV   Standard Reports in FICO

*Get introduced to **Standard Reports** in SAP FICO*

∞

Standard Reports are reports that come with system predefined. As against standard reports you will find 'user defined reports', defined by system implementation or support team as required by the user and is unique to individual business entity.

SAP Menu Tree for Standard Reports

Standard reports appear within 'Information System' menu under the respective sub modules of FI and CO.

Reports in FI

Menu path: Accounting >> Financial Accounting >> General Ledger >> Information System

i) General Ledger Reports >> Account Balances >> General >> GL Account Balances

S_ALR_87012277 - G/L Account Balances

ii) General Ledger Reports >> Line Items >> General Ledger Line Items

S_ALR_87012282 - G/L Line Items, List for Printing

Reports in CO

Menu path: Accounting >> Controlling >> Cost Center Accounting >> Information System >> Reports for Cost Center Accounting

i) Reports for Cost Center Accounting >> **Plan /Actual Comparisons**

S_ALR_87013611 - Cost Centers: Actual/Plan/Variance

ii) Reports for Cost Center Accounting >> **Actual /Actual Comparisons**

S_ALR_87013623 - Cost Centers: Quarterly Comparison

iii) Reports for Cost Center Accounting >> **Target /Actual Comparisons**

S_ALR_87013625 - Cost Centers: Actual/Target/Variance

The above report transaction codes along with menu path are only few of the available reports. I encourage you to explore further to see and use more reports that are available in the system.

∞∞

Chapter V Navigation in SAP [Part-II]

*Navigation in SAP FICO put YOU at **complete ease** with SAP Navigation*

*and a strong footing to move forward **confidently***

∞

1. Menu Bar and Application Tool Bar, How they change with Different Applications

Knowing what is Menu Bar and Application Tool Bar is a prerequisite for this chapter. To refresh please revisit: SAP Screen Structure Page 3 .

In a way, each module in SAP is a bundle of well knit Applications and Programs. Applications have unique functions. Application Tool Bar Icons or Menu Bar menu options for a given Application are available to cater to the respective functions. Navigation is learning to go to the desired Application and using the menu options and icons.

Step 1: SAP Easy Access screen. The first screen as you log in the system.

Step 2: Document entry or posting screen. Data entry screen for entering transactions in the system.

Step 3: Selection screen or parameter entry screen. When you want to run a report, you need to provide the selection parameters for the report to the system in a Selection screen.

Step 4: List screen. As you enter the parameters in a selection screen and run a report system generates the list of transactions in a list screen.

Step 5: Report screen. As you enter the parameters in a selection screen and run a report system generates the report in a report screen. Difference between a list and report is discussed later in this section.

Important: 'System' and 'Help' menu options remain in all applications.

Step 1: SAP Easy Access Screen

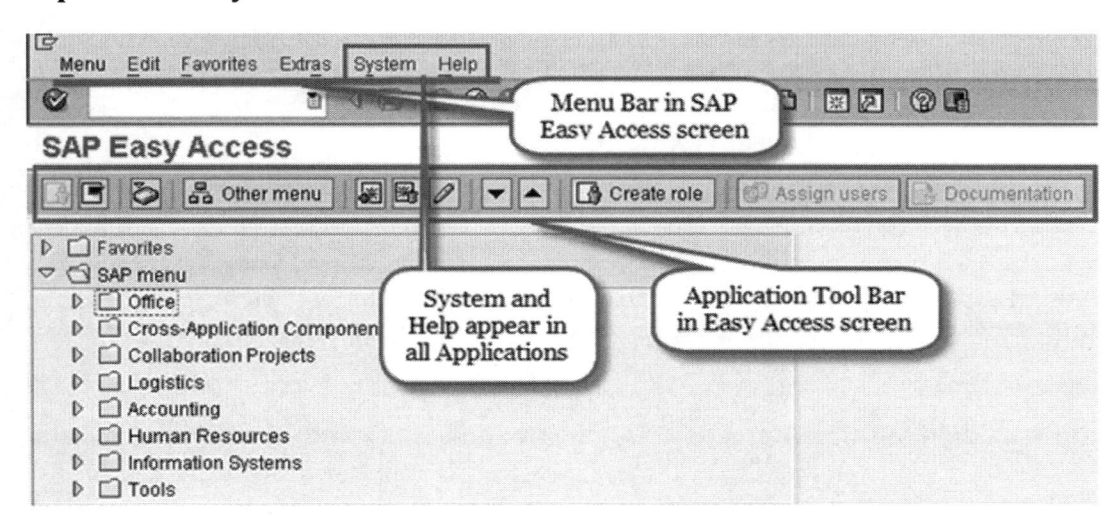

[Screenshot of SAP Easy Access screen with callouts: "Menu Bar in SAP Easy Access screen", "System and Help appear in all Applications", "Application Tool Bar in Easy Access screen". Menu shows: Favorites, SAP menu (Office, Cross-Application Components, Collaboration Projects, Logistics, Accounting, Human Resources, Information Systems, Tools)]

This is the first screen in the system as you log in SAP.

'Menu' Options: Click 'Menu' to open a) User menu b) SAP Menu and c) Business Workplace

a) User menu: This is set by your System Administrator. In case you cannot find a transaction or report in user menu, you can search for it in SAP Standard Menu.

b) SAP Menu: This is the standard SAP menu. This is built in a user-friendly logical hierarchy of system components or modules (Page 3).

c) Business Workplace /Cntl + F12

Application Tool Bar Icon:

Icon to go to 'Business Workplace', where you have the workflow functions for your user ID when you are part of the workflow defined in the SAP system. For example, you are the Finance Manager responsible to approve a budget for Admin. Once the draft admin budget is compiled, it will be forwarded to your 'workplace inbox' for approval. Business workplace contains inbox, outbox, resubmission, private folder and shared folder.

'Edit' Options: Click 'Edit' to open a) Execute in new window, b) Create shortcut on the Desktop.

a) Execute in new window /Ctrl + F2: After selecting the transaction in the SAP Menu, say, FB50 - Enter G/L Account Document, you can choose Edit >> Execute in new window, the transaction opens in new session.

b) Create Shortcut on the Desktop: Choose your often-used transaction in the menu and select this option under Edit. Desktop Shortcut for the transaction is defined. More discussion in Page 60.

Favorites: For grouping often used transaction codes, facilitating quicker navigation to the desired transaction. For more discussion, refer to Page 58.

Application Tool Bar Icons: for add, delete and change favorites.

Extras: You have a) Settings and b) Set Start Transaction.

a) Settings: Display technical names in SAP Menu. Discussed under Display TCodes in SAP Menu Page 8.

System and Help menus

System and Help menus remain the same while you run different applications in SAP such as Document entry, Report, List and so on.

Step 2: Document Entry Screen

Screen for document entry or post a transaction in the system.

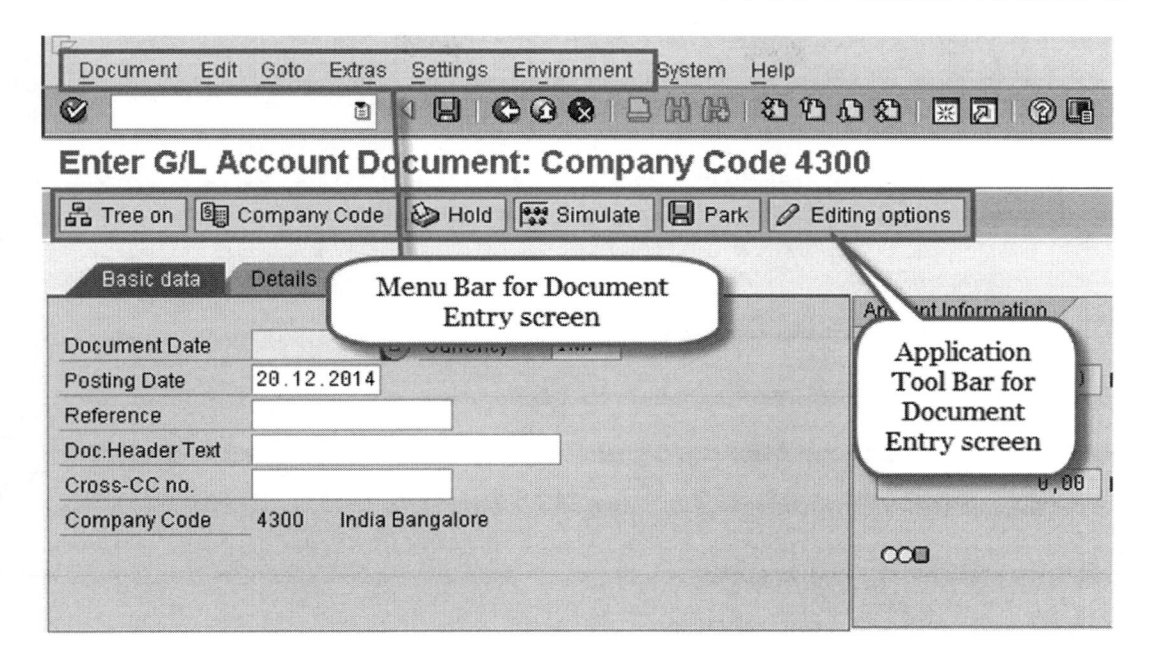

SAP FICO BEGINNER'S HANDBOOK 41

[Screenshot of Enter G/L Account Document: Company Code 4300 screen, with callouts labeling "Menu Bar for Document Entry screen" and "Application Tool Bar for Document Entry screen". Posting Date: 20.12.2014, Company Code: 4300 India Bangalore]

TCode used: FB50 - Enter G/L Account Document

Menu path: Accounting >> Financial Accounting >> General Ledger >> Posting

Enter the above TCode in command window and press 'Enter'. System takes you to Document Entry /Posting screen.

Menu Bar menus

When you are doing a Document Entry the Menu bar options will be <u>Document, Edit, Goto, Extras, Settings, Environment, System & Help</u>.

Menu Bar: Document >> Park /F8

Application Tool Bar: [Park icon]

Park icon, during Document entry you can 'park' the entry. Parked entry is in 'un-posted' status. When you want the entry to be checked by your colleague you can park an entry. It can be <u>posted</u> after the checking.

While running a report by default the report does not include parked transactions. When you want the report to include parked entries, enable Parked Documents under Further Selections in the 'Selection screen'.

Menu Bar: Document >> Simulate /F9

Application Tool Bar: [Simulate]

Simulate icon in Document entry screen to check if the entry is right.

Menu Bar: Settings >> Editing Options

Application Tool Bar: [Editing options]

SAP system offers many options to choose how you need the data entry screen to default values such as currency etc. Usually the default settings in 'Editing options' are good enough.

Step 3: Selection Screen

Screen to make parameter selections when you run a report.

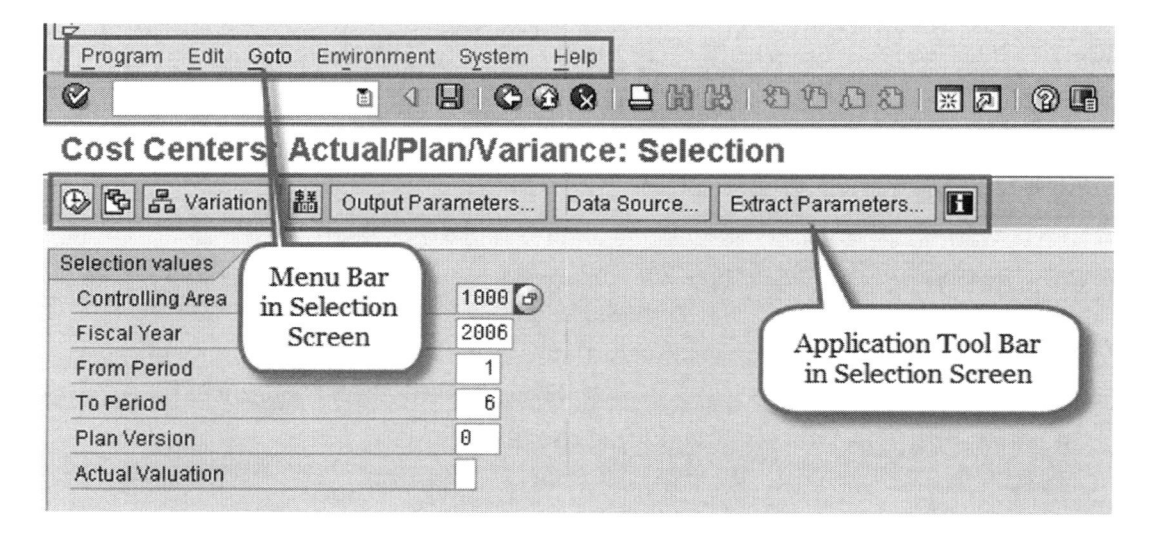

TCode used: S_ALR_87013611 - Cost Centers: Actual/Plan/Variance

Menu path: Accounting >> Financial Accounting >> Controlling >> Cost Center Accounting >> Information System >> Reports for Cost Center Accounting >> Plan Actual Comparisons

System takes you to the Selection Screen.

Menu Bar

When you are in a Parameter Selection Screen for say, Running a Report, the Menu bar options will be <u>Program, Edit, Goto, Environment, System & Help</u>.

Execute

Menu Bar: Program >> Execute /F8

Application Tool Bar:

This icon is used to execute the program in the system. You need to enter valid parameters in data entry fields in the Selection Screen and click this icon to get the report.

Once the required values, called 'parameters' are entered in the respective data entry fields of the Selection Screen, you can 'Execute' using menu path 'Program >> Execute' or click 'Execute' Icon in the 'Application Tool Bar' or hit F8 to run the program and get the report.

Background Processing

Menu Bar: Program >> Execute in Background

As against the above method, you can execute a program in the background. Background execution will be necessary when system takes longer time to fetch the required data. This can happen when the particular program is data intensive.

Under this circumstance, you have the option to schedule the program to run at a time when system resources are used to the minimum, say after office hours.

System prompts you to choose printer, enter date and time to execute the report.

Important: There is no icon for background processing.

44 SAP FICO BEGINNER'S HANDBOOK

Variants

Menu Bar: Go To >> Variants >> Get /Shift + F5

Application Tool Bar:

You can define and save the often used 'selection screen data entry field values' as 'Selection Variant' in the system. For further discussion, please refer page 84.

Step 4: List screen

List is a form of SAP report.

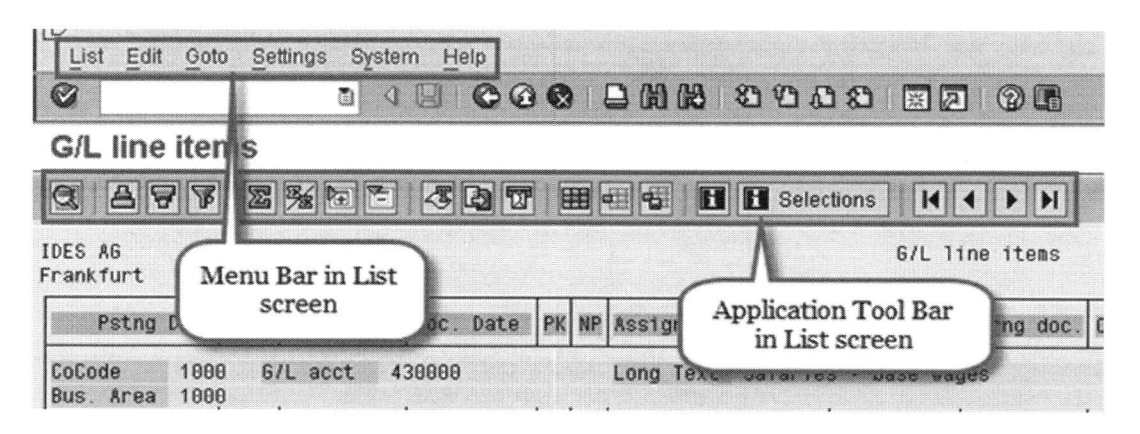

TCode Used: S_ALR_87012282 - G/L Line Items, List for Printing

Menu path: Accounting >> Financial Accounting >> General Ledger >> Information System >> General Ledger Reports (New) >> Line Items

Input valid data in Selection Screen for the above TCode and click Execute icon or hit F8. System takes you to the List display screen.

Menu Bar

When a List is generated through a Parameter Selection Screen, the Menu bar options will be List, Edit, Goto, Settings, System & Help.

Filter

Menu Bar: Edit >> Set Filter

Application Tool Bar:

You can choose a column, say 'Amount in LC' (amount in local currency) and set a filter 'greater than, say 13,000'. This will produce a report with line items with only 'Amount in LC' greater than 13,000.

List items can be 'Filtered' at multi level and even on a hidden field. For a detailed discussion, please refer page 102.

Sort

Menu Bar: Edit >> Sort in Ascending / Sort in Descending

Application Tool Bar:

When you generate a Report, system will display data in columnar form. Consider you want the entire report data to be sorted in say, ascending order of column, say Invoice Amt. Then choose 'Invoice Amt' Column and click 'Ascending' Icon. The displayed data is sorted per your requirement, lowest invoice amount line item at the top.

For a detailed discussion on sort function, which is very useful, please refer to page 99.

Total

Menu Bar: Edit >> Total

Application Tool Bar:

Please note 'Total' of columns having amounts is displayed by default. However if you do not want the 'Total' displayed select the respective column and click this icon.

This is a toggle button, by selecting the respective column and clicking again the 'Total' button system will display the 'Total' values.

Subtotals

Menu Bar: Edit >> Subtotals

46 SAP FICO BEGINNER'S HANDBOOK

Application Tool Bar:

While in a 'List', you can enable subtotal based on chosen field value. For more details, please refer to page 104.

Layout

Menu Bar: Settings >> Layout >> Change /Choose/ Save

Application Tool Bar:

You can change the layout of a report; say, selecting columns to display or hide, defining column width and much more. Once your layout is defined, you can assign a name and save the defined layout for later use.

Please refer to page 92 for a narrative explanation.

Step 5: Report screen

Report screen presents another form of report. We will discuss later about difference between a list and a report.

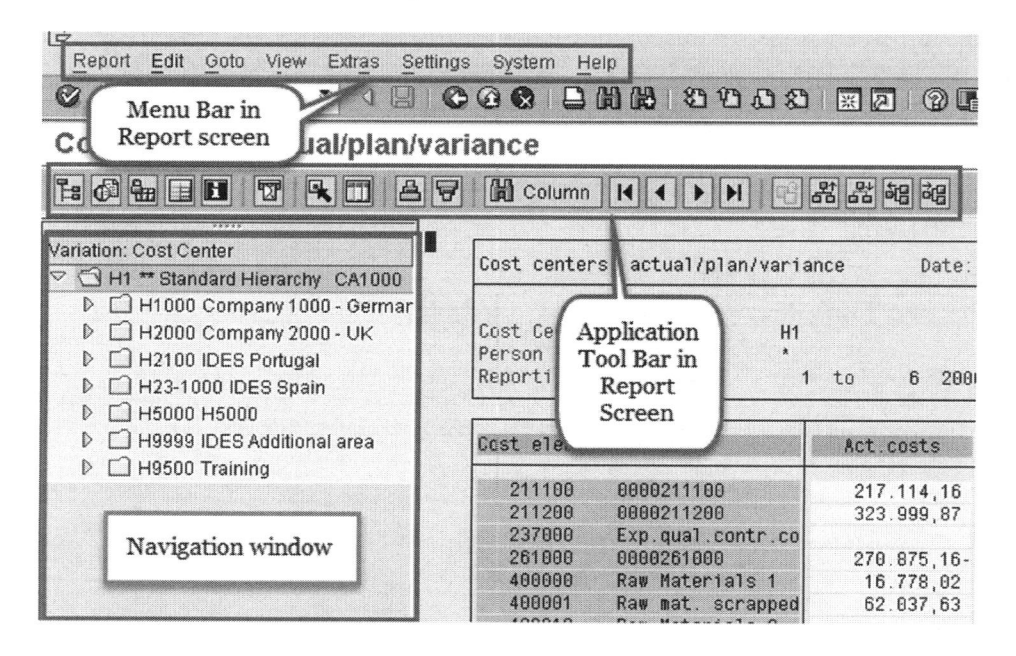

TCode used: Code S_ALR_87013611 - Cost Centers: Actual/Plan/Variance

Input valid data in Selection Screen for the above TCode and click 'Execute' icon or hit F8. System takes you to the 'Report' display screen.

Navigation Window

Application Tool Bar: Navigation on /off: When you run the report for a cost center group, you have the option to view the report either for the CC group or for individual cost centers using a navigation window to the left of the report. You can hide or unhide the navigation window using this icon. There is no equivalent option in menu bar for this function.

Options

Menu path: Settings >> Options

Application Tool Bar:

You can enable Expert mode check box if you want to manage Report Extracts. Please follow to page 119 for a detailed discussion on Extracts.

You can enable MS Excel for reports for displaying report data in Excel within SAP.

Call up reports

Menu path: Edit >> Call up report /F7

Application Tool Bar:

It is a report interface option. You can run related reports (branch out) directly from this report without further parameter selections. Parameter already selected for the running report would be applied for the report you are branching out.

For a given report there are 10 related reports as under:

1. Cost Centers: Actual Line Items
2. Cost Centers: Planning Overview
3. Cost Centers: Plan Line Items
4. CCtrs: Period breakdown actual/plan

5. Activity Types: Period Breakdown
6. Stat. Key Figs: Period breakdown
7. Cost Centers: Breakdown by Partner
8. Cost centers: Breakdown by transactions
9. Area: Actual/plan 2 currencies
10. Display Planning Long Texts

Prerequisite: To get related report you need to select one report item. Say 400000 Raw Materials and run report 1. Cost Centers: Actual Line Items.

Difference between Report & List

- From a Report you can drill down to transaction level where as this is not usually available for a List
- Normally you don't have the option to change 'Layout' in a Report where as Layout can be changed for a List
- Report is produced by aggregating data like cost for a cost element in a given period. Whereas List is transaction data fetched without any aggregation

∞

2. Exporting report to Excel, Word, Mail

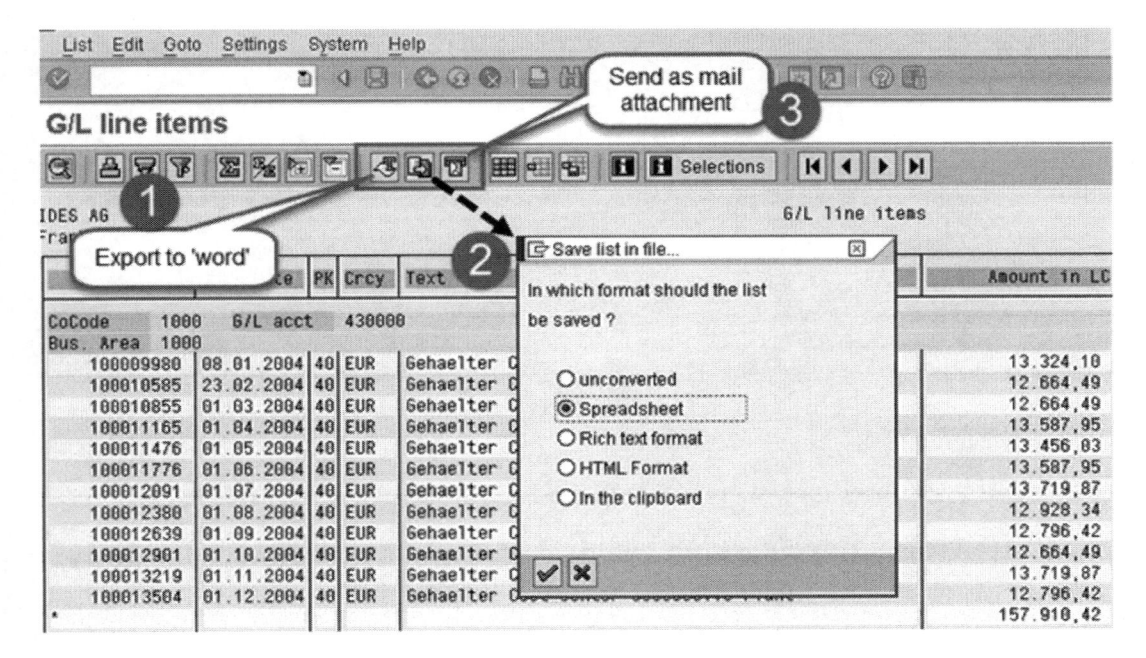

1. Exporting to Word: Click 'Word Processing' Icon /Ctrl+Shift+F8

2. To export to MS Excel or Clipboard: Click 'Local File' Icon /Ctrl+Shift+F9. Report copied to clipboard can be pasted to an Excel or Word file.

3. Menu path: Report >> Send

To send as mail attachment via the SAP mail option: Click 'Mail Recipient' /Ctrl+F7. The List as attachment can be sent to an external mail address or to an SAP Logon name.

3. Standard Tool Bar Icons

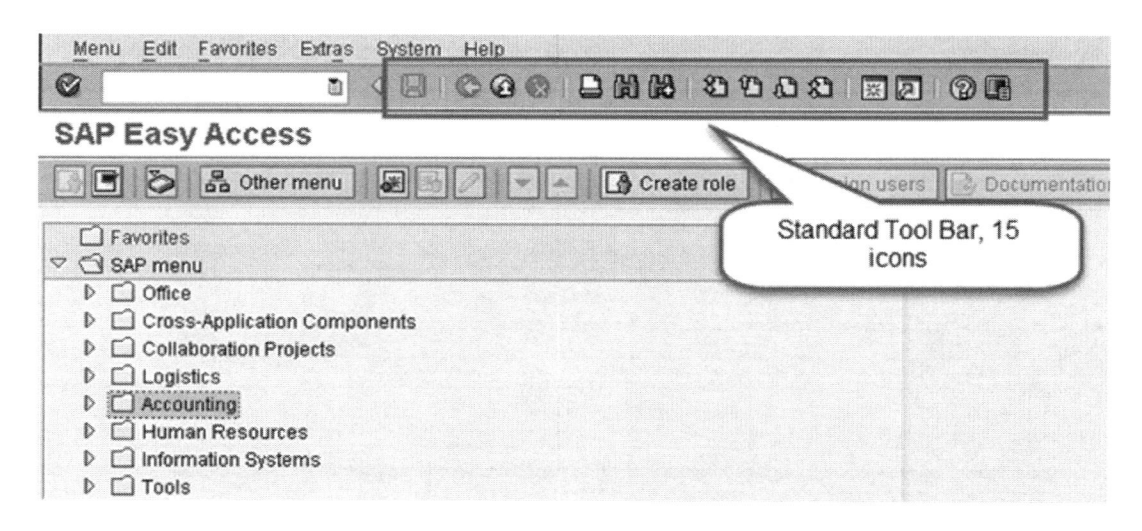

[Screenshot of SAP Easy Access screen with Standard Tool Bar highlighted and labeled "Standard Tool Bar, 15 icons"]

Unlike Menu Bar and Application Tool Bar, Standard Tool Bar remains constant irrespective of what application you run in SAP system. However if an icon is not applicable or not functional for a particular screen then that icon would appear as grayed out.

Example: Post /Save as variant icon in SAP Easy Access screen.

Standard Tool Bar Icons

1. Post /Save as variant /Cntl + S

Left-click on the Save button when you want to save data or save changes to data. For example you are in a data entry screen you can use this button to save the data.

Note, while in data entry this icon is 'Post' and in Selection Screen for running a report this icon is 'Save as variant'

This icon is grayed out when there is nothing to Post or Save.

2. Back /F3

Left-click on the Back button to move back to the previous screen or previous menu level.

3. Log off, Exit /Shift + F3

Left-click the Exit button when you want to exit the current menu level or system task <u>without saving</u> the data. When in a system task the icon is Exit, to leave the task and return to the previous window. When in initial screen this is <u>Log off</u> to exit the SAP system.

4. Cancel /F12

Left-click on the Cancel button when you want to cancel the data you entered in a data entry field.

5. Print /Cntl + P

Left-click on the Print button to print the SAP document displayed on the screen.

6, 7. Find /Cntl + F, Find next /Cntl + G

Left-click on the Find button (binoculars) when you want the system to search for words and alphanumeric combinations in the 'List or Report' screen.

Use the Find next button (the binoculars with + sign) to continue searching for a previously selected search item.

8. First Page /Cntl + Page up

Left-click on the double-arrow up button to move to the first page of a <u>multi page 'List or Report'</u> screen.

9. Previous Page /Page up

Left-click on the single-arrow up button to move to the previous page.

10. Next Page /Page Down

Left-click on the single-arrow down button to move to the next page.

11. Last Page /Cntl + Page Down

Left-click on the double-arrow down to move to the last page of a multi page 'List or Report' screen.

12. New Session

Discussed under Working with Multiple Sessions Page 7.

13. Generate a Shortcut

Left-click on the Shortcut button to generate a shortcut on your desktop, Page 60.

14. Help /F1

The Yellow question mark is the Help button. It displays Generic SAP Online Help.

15. Customize Local Layout /Alt + F12

You can Customize SAP Layout, (page 70) the way information, warning and error messages are displayed.

∞

4. Display TCodes in SAP Menu

SAP Menu is arranged in a logical hierarchy. By default, SAP Menu displays only the 'Description' and NOT the technical names of the Transaction Codes.

Why we want the TCodes in the SAP Menu?

It helps to memorize the respective TCode for a given transaction. Once the TCode is known the same can be entered in the Command Window to increase your navigation speed.

To enable the system display TCodes in the Menu Tree, follow the steps:

Step1

Menu path: 'Extras >> Settings'. 'Settings' window pops up.

Step2

Enable 'Display technical names'. Now the Menu shows the TCodes.

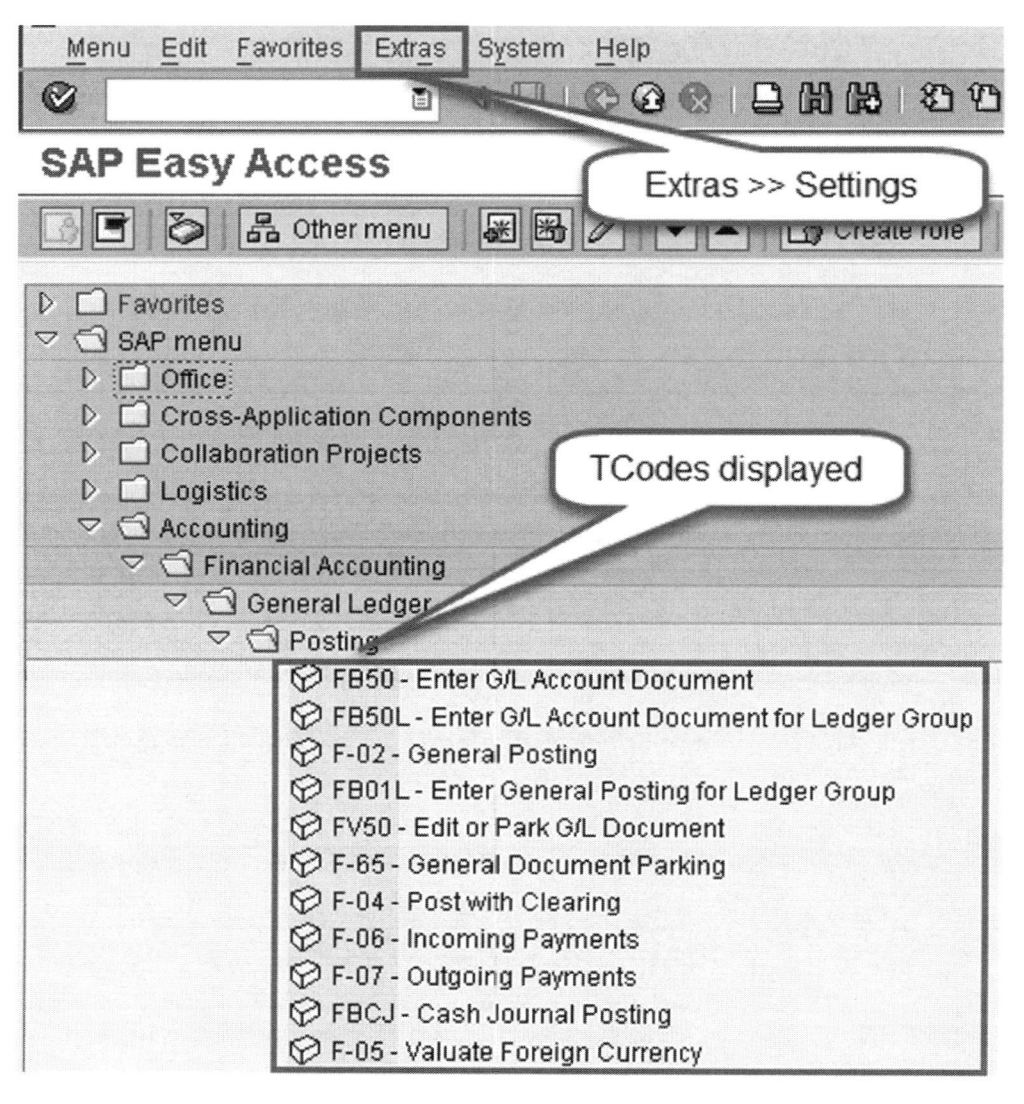

54 SAP FICO BEGINNER'S HANDBOOK

Extras >> Settings

TCodes displayed

- Favorites
- SAP menu
  - Office
  - Cross-Application Components
  - Collaboration Projects
  - Logistics
  - Accounting
    - Financial Accounting
      - General Ledger
        - Posting
          - FB50 - Enter G/L Account Document
          - FB50L - Enter G/L Account Document for Ledger Group
          - F-02 - General Posting
          - FB01L - Enter General Posting for Ledger Group
          - FV50 - Edit or Park G/L Document
          - F-65 - General Document Parking
          - F-04 - Post with Clearing
          - F-06 - Incoming Payments
          - F-07 - Outgoing Payments
          - FBCJ - Cash Journal Posting
          - F-05 - Valuate Foreign Currency

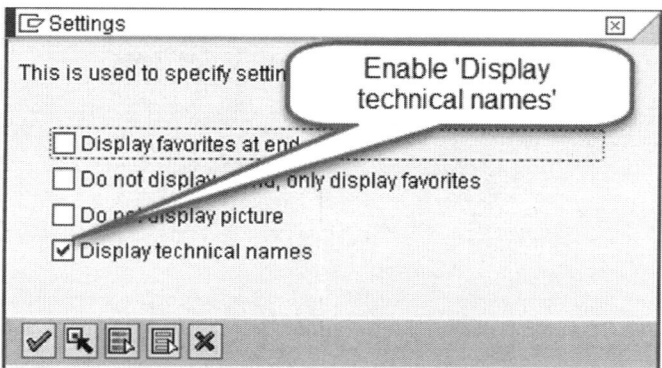

Enable 'Display technical names'

Settings
This is used to specify settin...
- ☐ Display favorites at end
- ☐ Do not display ..., only display favorites
- ☐ Do not display picture
- ☑ Display technical names

5. Status Bar for System Messages and Session Information

System Messages

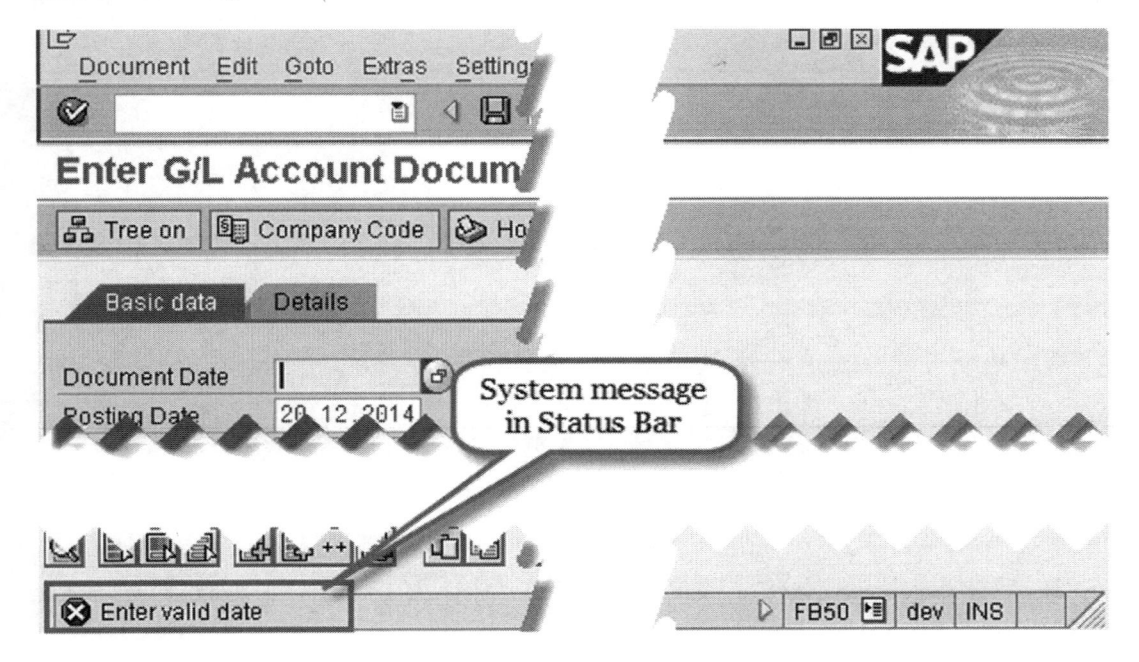

Status bar has two sections. <u>left</u> side and <u>right</u> side. On the left side, SAP System displays program messages like error, warning, transaction saved and so on. So **while executing a transaction, watch this bar** for system message to make sure, if the transaction is through or it failed.

Session Information Display

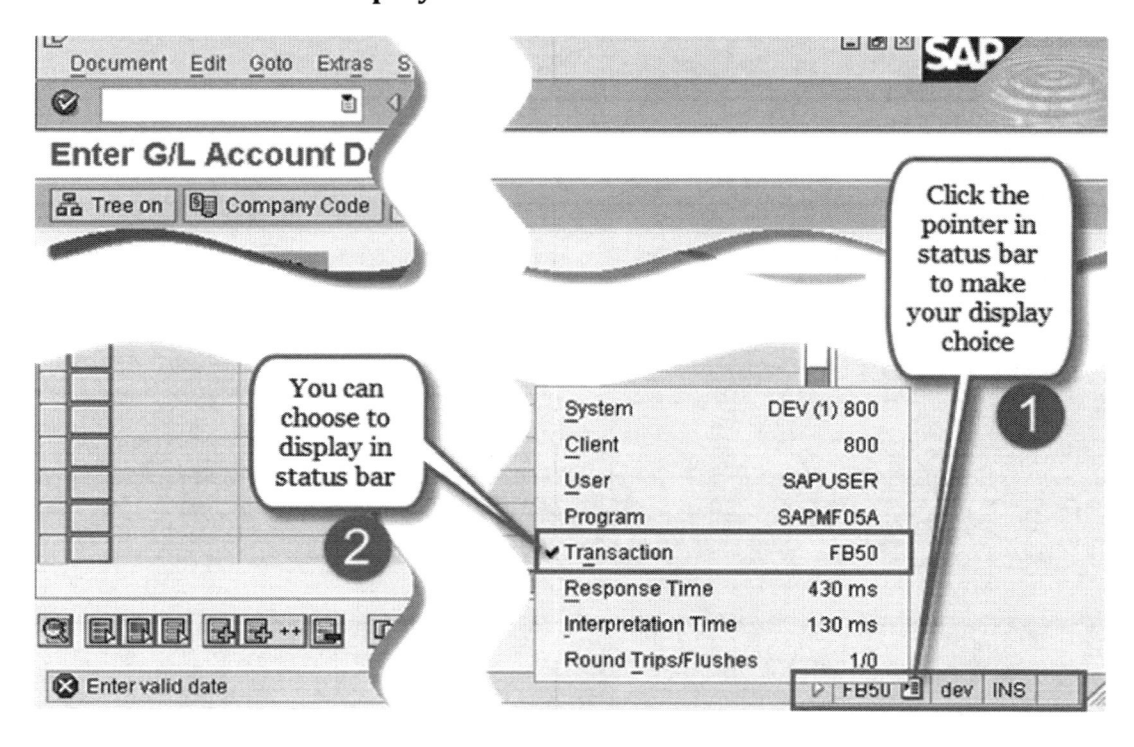

Right side of Status Bar you can see information about the system status like program name, Transaction Code etc as per your preference.

6. Homework for you!

Give a man a fish and you feed him for a day;

teach a man to fish and you feed him for a lifetime

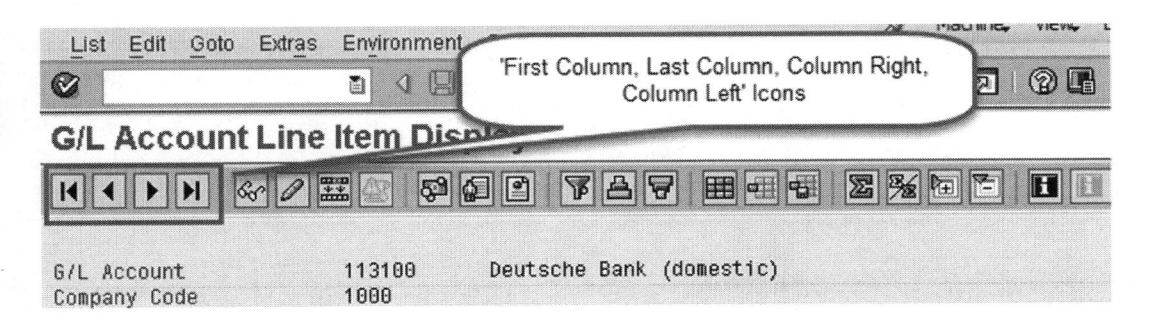

∞

Run Transaction Code FBL3N - Display/Change Line Items, and choose your parameters to run the report.

Home work 1

Explore 'First Column, Last Column, Column Right, Column Left' Icons.

Home work 2

Select one of the columns (not the right most column).

Follow menu path: Settings >> Columns >> Freeze to Column.

Now again explore the 'First Column, Last Column, Column Right, Column Left' Icons.

Before we move on to the next chapter

The chapter on 'Navigation' would have put you on strong pedestal to explore the system further. With the icons you learnt now, please do continue to learn the functionalities of new icons that you come across while working with SAP.

∞∞

Chapter VI   SAP Tips & Tricks

*Essential SAP Tips make YOUR SAP FICO **experience a pleasure***

∞

1. Favorites

You can bring together in one place called 'Favorites' all your favorite TCodes in SAP Menu. This is a good way of organizing TCodes and improving your navigation speed.

Application Tool Bar: Add, Delete, Change Favorites Icons

Menu path: (Menu Bar) Favorites >> Add, Delete, Change

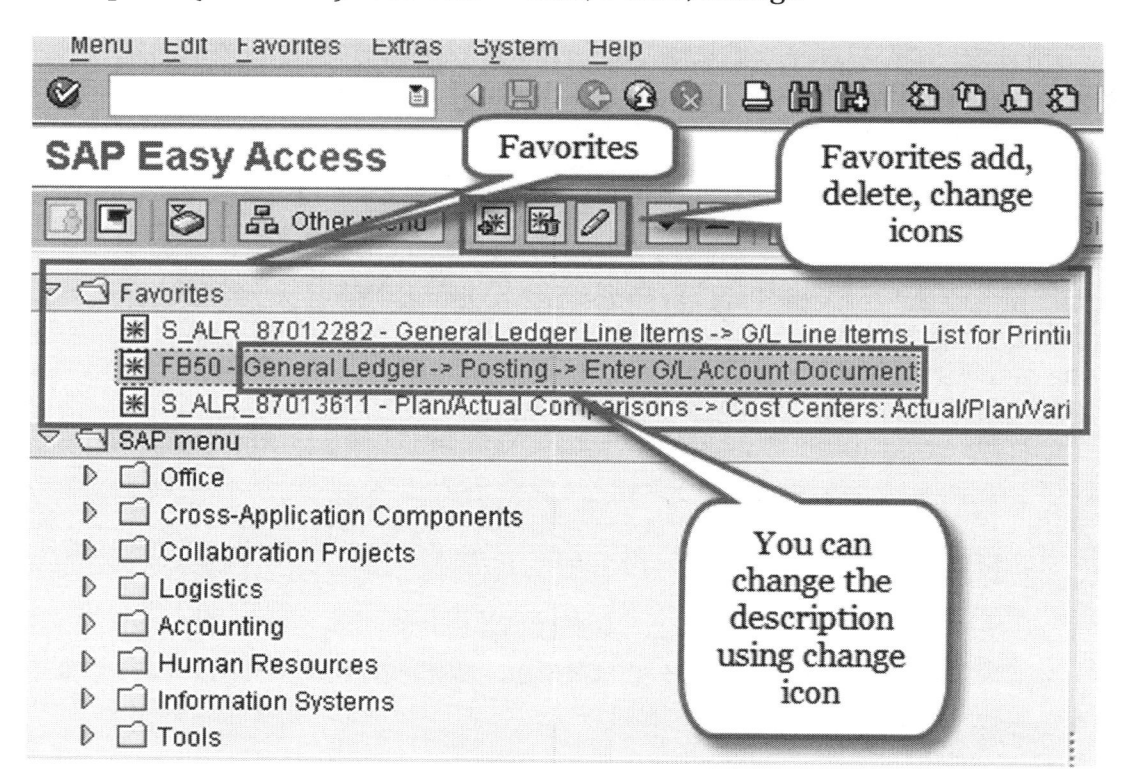

You can keep your often-used SAP Menu Items in 'Favorites', just above 'SAP Menu'. This helps you to quickly go to the transaction or report window of your choice.

You can add a chosen SAP Menu item either by right click and choose 'Add to Favorites' or using the Menu 'Favorites'.

You can change the TCode <u>description</u>. Choose the item already in Favorites and follow menu path <u>Favorites >> Change</u>.

You can also create 'Folders' with suitable names and arrange your chosen SAP Menu items under the respective folders. Organized this way minimizes time to select and run a TCode.

∞

60 SAP FICO BEGINNER'S HANDBOOK

2. Desktop Shortcut for SAP Transaction

We use 'Desktop Shortcuts' for our day-to-day applications like MS Word, MS Excel and PowerPoint. In the same way, we can create Desktop Shortcuts for Transaction Codes.

Let us consider that one of your daily routines include Cash Journal Entries. We log in SAP, type the TCode **FBCJ** in command field or follow menu path: Accounting >> Financial Accounting >> General Ledger >> Posting >> Cash Journal Posting.

To make your life simpler, let us create a Desktop Shortcut for TCode **FBCJ**.

Go to the transaction screen for which you want to create the Shortcut. Follow menu path as above or type FBCJ in command field and press enter.

Choose Customize Local Layout icon, the last icon in the Standard Toolbar (Alt+F12).

Click Create Shortcut.

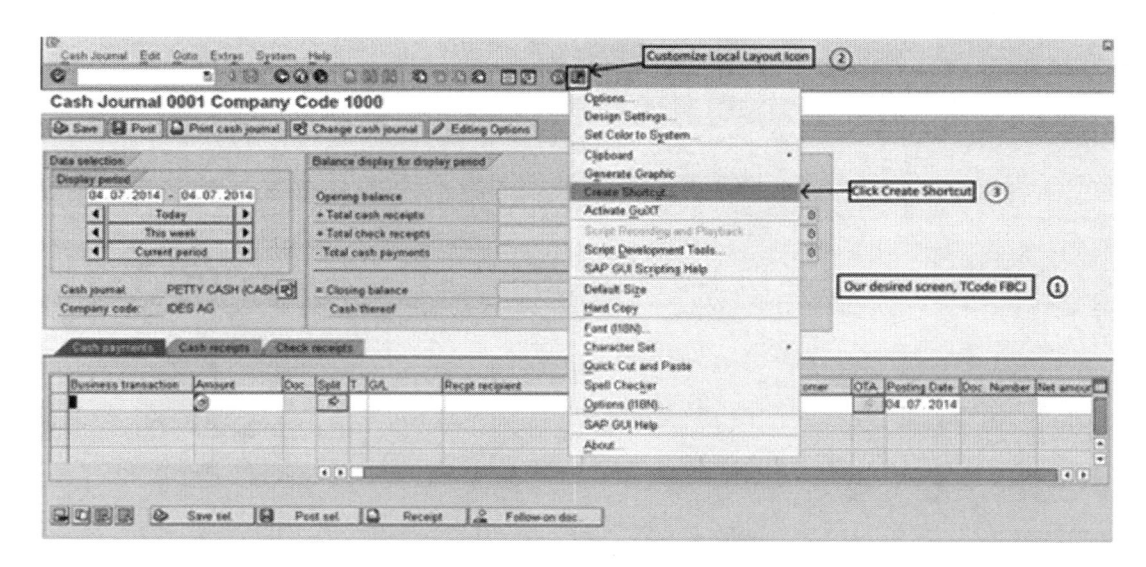

As you have started from the chosen transaction screen, 'Cash Journal', SAP R/3 system has already populated the entry fields with defaults:

- Title
- Type

SAP FICO BEGINNER'S HANDBOOK 61

- Transaction
- System Description
- Client
- User
- Password - It is recommended to <u>leave this blank</u>
- Language
- Location - where we need the Shortcut Icon, 'Desktop'
- Click Finish

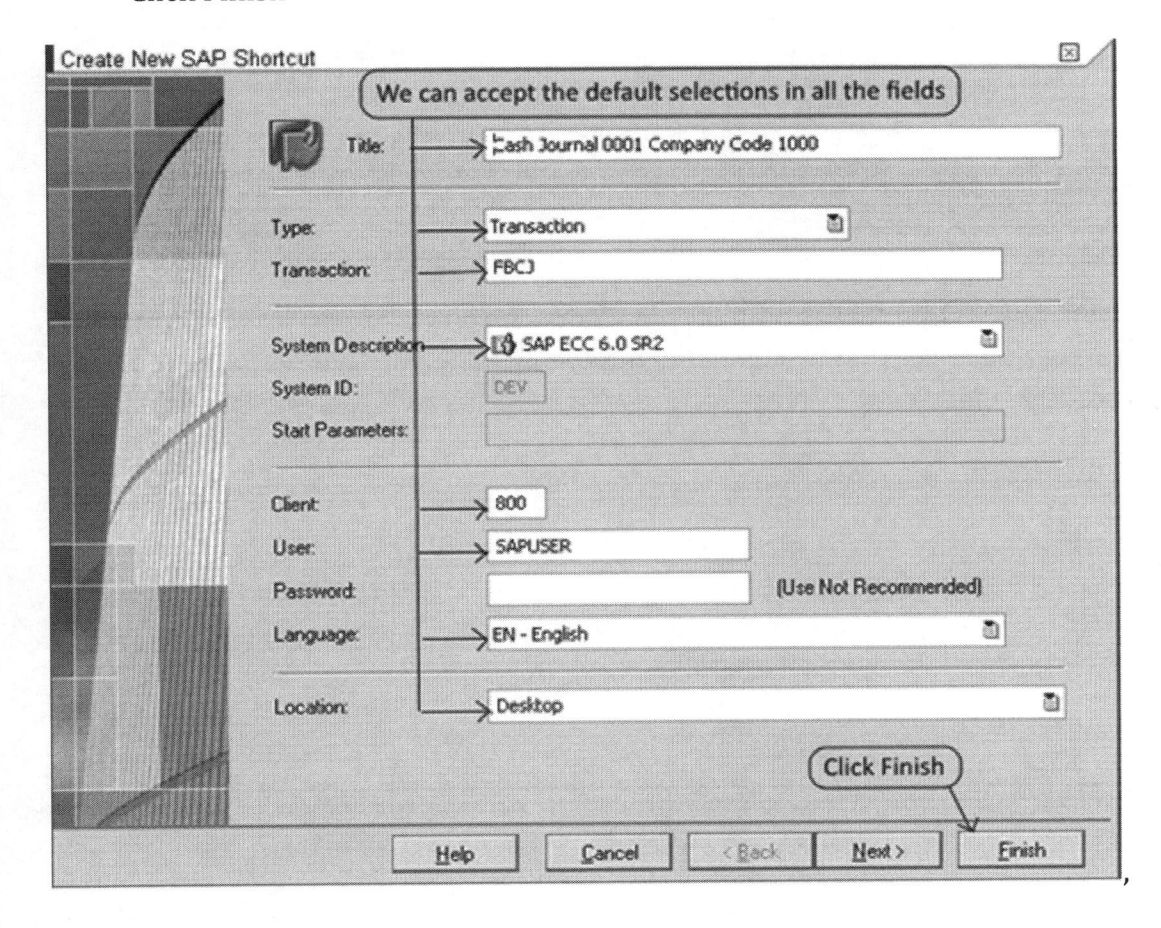

![Create New SAP Shortcut dialog: We can accept the default selections in all the fields. Title: Cash Journal 0001 Company Code 1000; Type: Transaction; Transaction: FBCJ; System Description: SAP ECC 6.0 SR2; System ID: DEV; Client: 800; User: SAPUSER; Password: (Use Not Recommended); Language: EN - English; Location: Desktop. Click Finish.]

The shortcut icon is created in your Desktop. Next time when you log on SAP and go to your daily routine, 'Cash Journal', you can click the Desk Top shortcut created and enter your password. You are taken to the Cash Journal entry screen directly!

Set Start Transaction

Do you want your 'system log on icon' to take you to a particular transaction code, then follow menu path Extras >> Set Start Transaction.

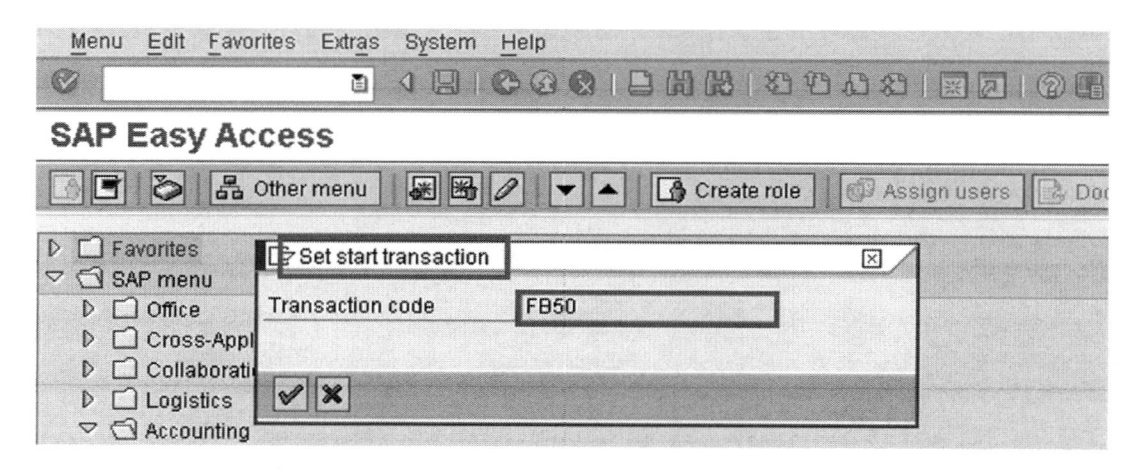

Enter the TCode, say FB50 in the dialog box and press 'Enter'. Your start transaction is set. Next time when you log on SAP, you will be directly taken to this TCode FB50!

∞

3. Finding Transaction Code in SAP Menu

Consider you want to know the menu path where a given Transaction Code, say 'MIRO' is placed in SAP Menu. Press 'Cntl + F' and enter 'MIRO', check 'In Technical Name' and uncheck 'in Texts' and press 'Enter'. You will be taken to the MIRO TCode in the SAP Menu.

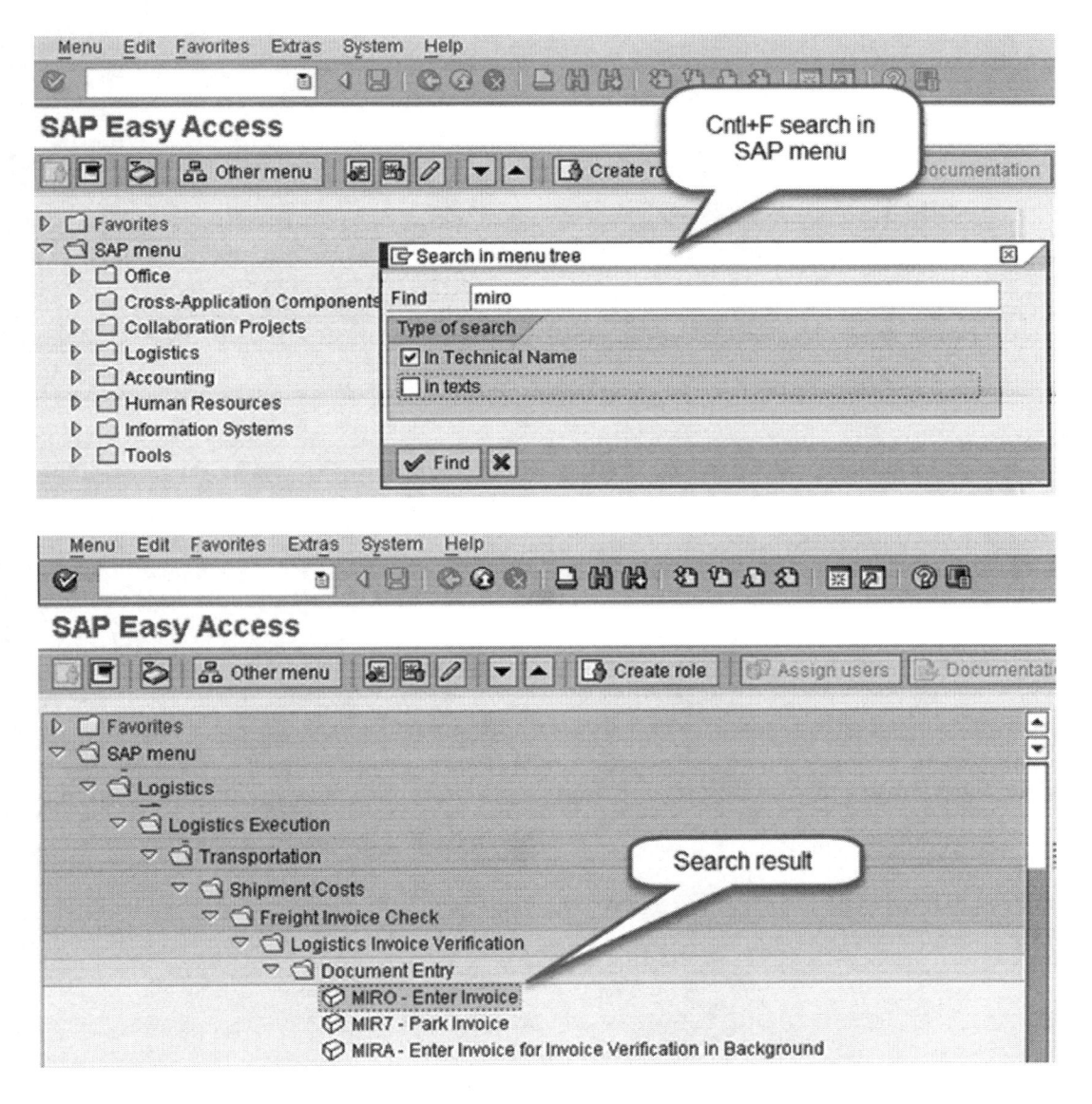

In the same way you can do a search based on 'text', say 'average costs'. Uncheck 'in Technical Terms' and check 'in texts' check box and press 'Enter'. You will be taken to the Transaction Code containing description 'average costs'. This way

64 SAP FICO BEGINNER'S HANDBOOK

you can find out the TCode for a know text description of the transaction that you want to run.

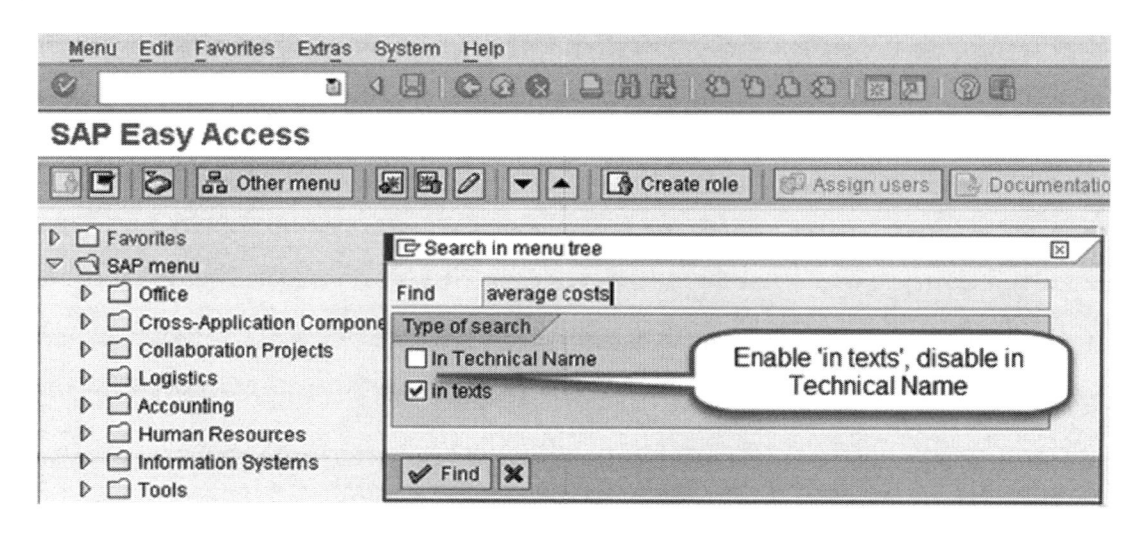

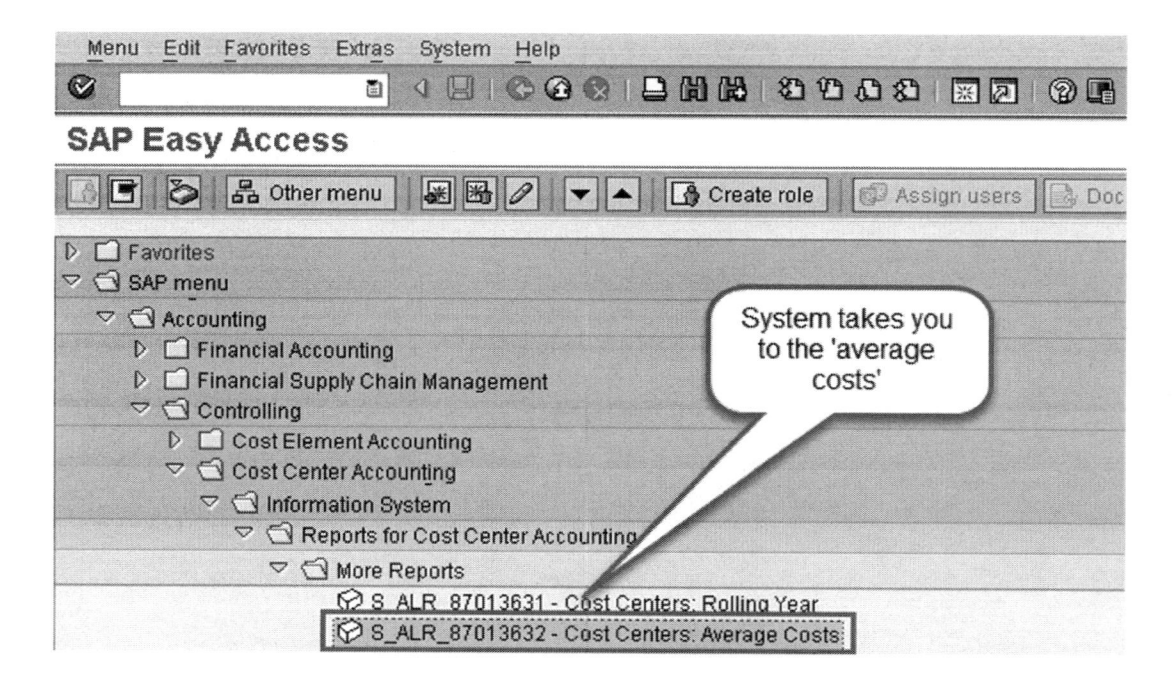

Note: Enabling or disabling 'in Technical Name' and 'in texts' is to improve system performance only. Enabling both options will also produce same results, only system takes more time.

SAP FICO BEGINNER'S HANDBOOK 65

4. Using Tab Options and Personal Value List in F4 help

What is F4 help or F4 selection?

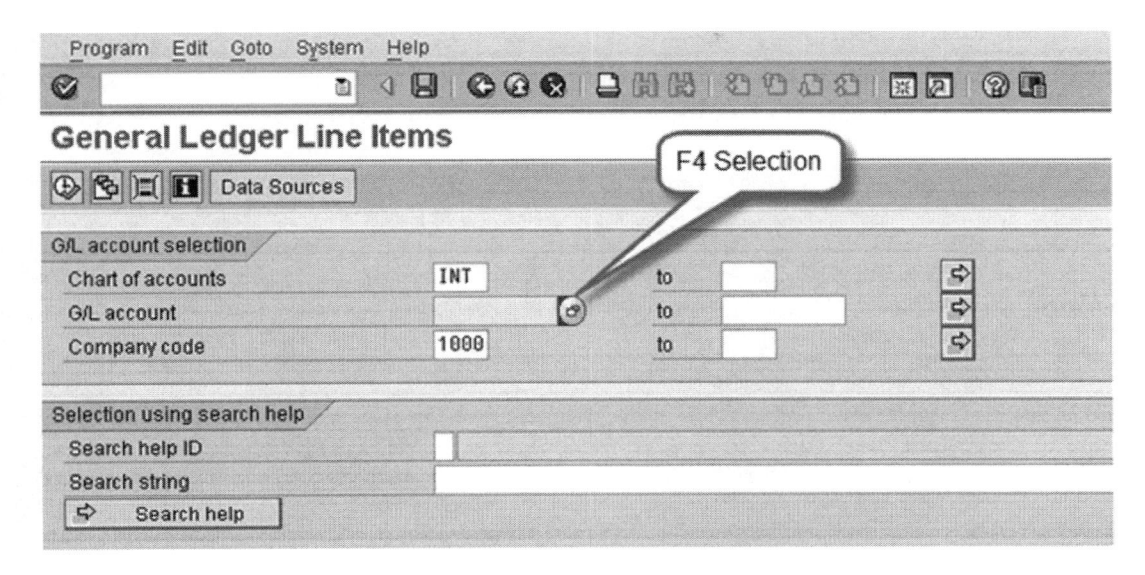

[Screenshot: General Ledger Line Items screen with F4 Selection button highlighted on G/L account field]

Most data entry fields you have the 'F4 Selection' button. This button appears once your cursor is in the field for data entry. In case you do not have the value to enter this field, press F4 or click this button to take system help to get the data for the field.

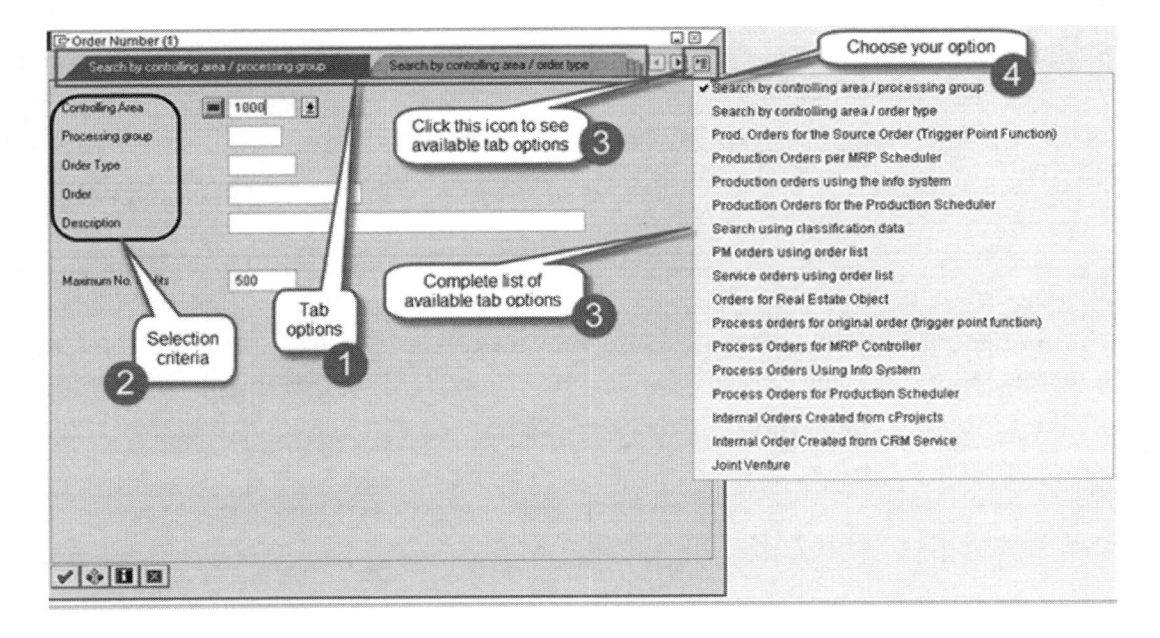

[Screenshot: Order Number (1) pop-up window showing Tab options, Selection criteria, and a list of search options including "Search by controlling area / processing group", "Search by controlling area / order type", "Prod. Orders for the Source Order (Trigger Point Function)", "Production Orders per MRP Scheduler", "Production orders using the info system", "Production Orders for the Production Scheduler", "Search using classification data", "PM orders using order list", "Service orders using order list", "Orders for Real Estate Object", "Process orders for original order (trigger point function)", "Process Orders for MRP Controller", "Process Orders Using Info System", "Process Orders for Production Scheduler", "Internal Orders Created from cProjects", "Internal Order Created from CRM Service", "Joint Venture"]

F4 Selection takes you to the pop up window as in the picture.

66 SAP FICO BEGINNER'S HANDBOOK

1. This window comes with many 'Tab options'.
2. Each 'Tab option' provides one combination of 'Selection criteria' to help you choose the list of values for the data entry fields.
3. You can click the pointer at the right end of the Tab options to see all the available 'Tab options'
4. You can choose a 'Tab option' here to have the right 'Selection criteria'.

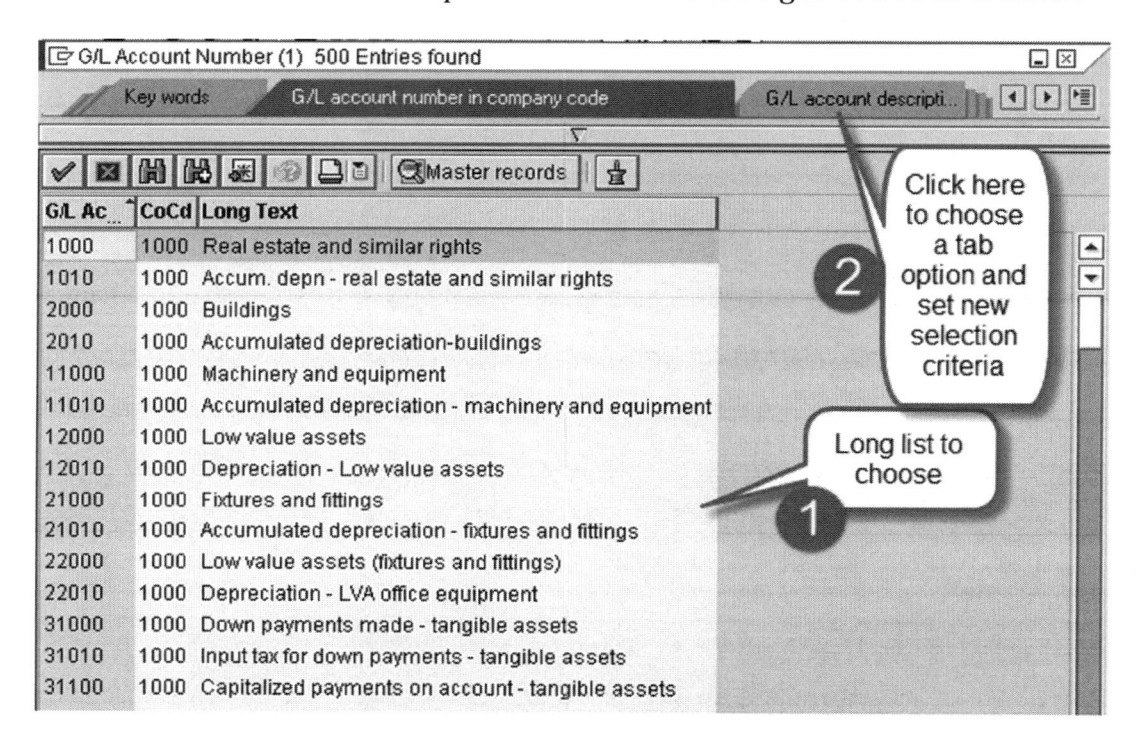

G/L Ac	CoCd	Long Text
1000	1000	Real estate and similar rights
1010	1000	Accum. depn - real estate and similar rights
2000	1000	Buildings
2010	1000	Accumulated depreciation-buildings
11000	1000	Machinery and equipment
11010	1000	Accumulated depreciation - machinery and equipment
12000	1000	Low value assets
12010	1000	Depreciation - Low value assets
21000	1000	Fixtures and fittings
21010	1000	Accumulated depreciation - fixtures and fittings
22000	1000	Low value assets (fixtures and fittings)
22010	1000	Depreciation - LVA office equipment
31000	1000	Down payments made - tangible assets
31010	1000	Input tax for down payments - tangible assets
31100	1000	Capitalized payments on account - tangible assets

Tabs: Key words | G/L account number in company code | G/L account descripti...

Callouts:
- Click here to choose a tab option and set new selection criteria (2)
- Long list to choose (1)

1. Say you have chosen 'Company code = 1000' in the 'Tab option' and press 'Enter' to get the above list. Yes, this is a big list. You need a smaller list that fit in your definition. Let us go to the next step.

2. In order to further limit this list you can select again the Tab option 'GL account description in company code' at the top of the list screen. Type, say '*wages*' (Note asterisk mark) against 'GL Account long description' and '1000' against 'Company code' and press 'Enter' to get a smaller list from which you can choose your GL Code.

Create Personal Value List

Choose your often used GL Account code say, Salaries -base wages, 430000 and click 'Personal value list' icon as shown in (2).

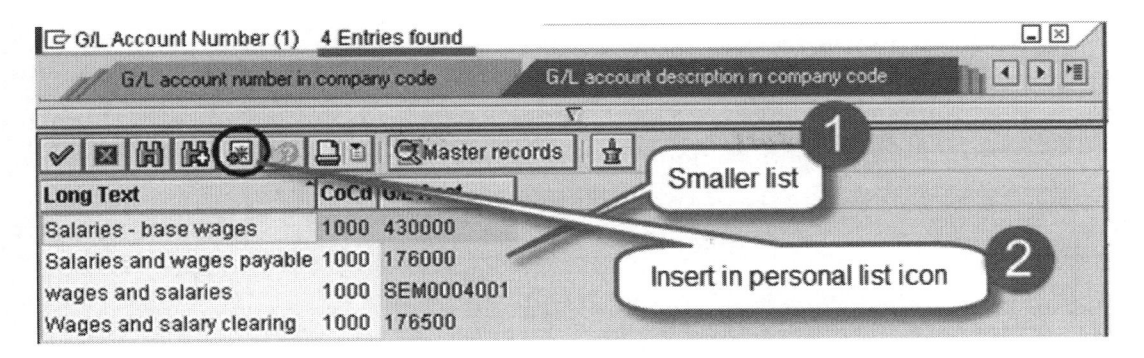

[G/L Account Number (1) screenshot showing 4 Entries found with columns Long Text, CoCd, G/L Account:
- Salaries - base wages | 1000 | 430000
- Salaries and wages payable | 1000 | 176000
- wages and salaries | 1000 | SEM0004001
- Wages and salary clearing | 1000 | 176500

Callouts: "Smaller list" (1), "Insert in personal list icon" (2)]

Next time when you press F4 for the 'GL account' data entry field you will be presented with your personal value list as in the picture. If you want to select GL account other than the Personal value list you can do so by clicking 'Tab option' at the top of the list window and make your choices. You can have one or more items in your Personal Value list.

[G/L Account Number (1) Personal Value List screenshot showing 1 Entry found:
- Salaries - base wages | 1000 | 430000

Callout: "Personal value list"]

You can delete the items in the personal value list or add new items to the list any time.

∞

68 SAP FICO BEGINNER'S HANDBOOK

5. Copy Paste in SAP

You want to do a copy paste in SAP. Consider a section of the SAP report which you want to copy to clipboard and paste it in an Excel file.

You can do this in four easy steps!

Step 1

After generating the report go to <u>copy mode</u> by typing 'Cntl+Y'. Your cursor becomes a hairline.

Step 2

Select the area you want to copy using 'cursor + mouse left click'.

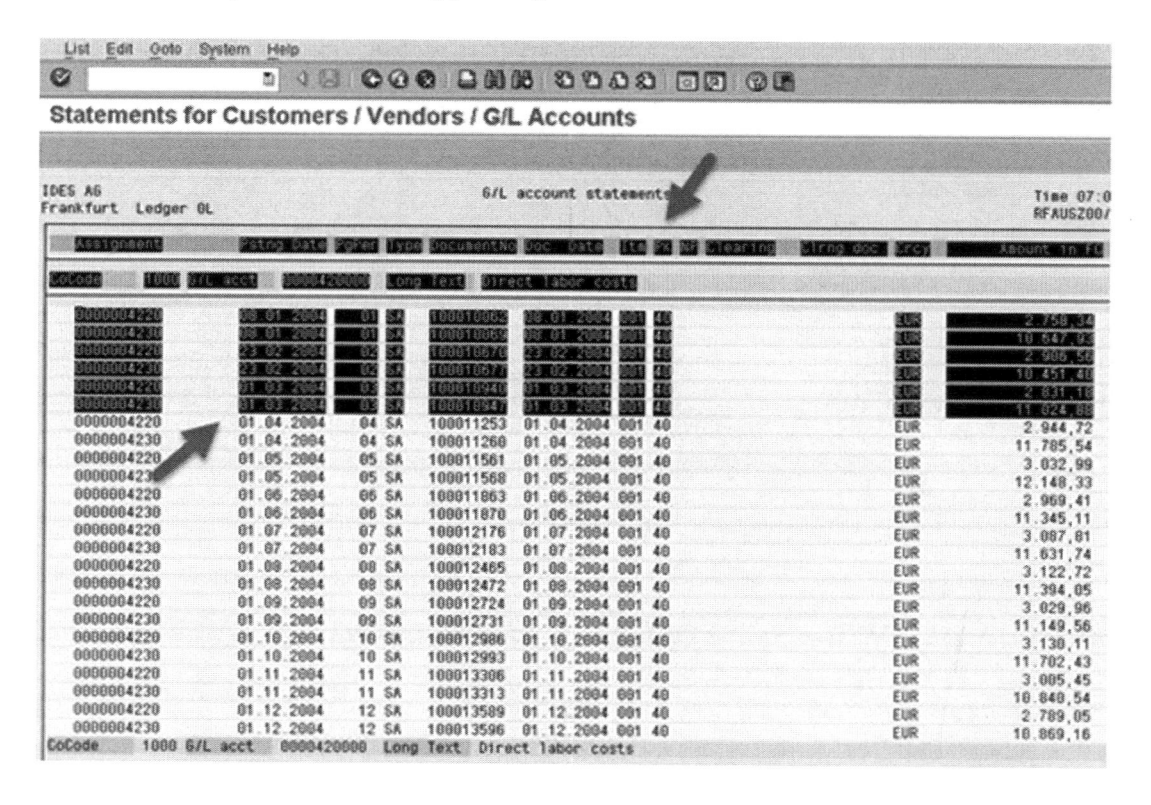

Step 3

Copy the selection to clipboard by typing 'Cntl+C'

Step 4

Go to Excel file where you want to copy the data, select a cell, press 'Cntl+V'.

	A	B	C	D	E	F	G	H	I	J	K	L	M
1													
2													
3		Assignment	Pstng Date	PgPer	Type	DocumentNo	Doc. Date	Itm	PK	NP Clearing	Clrng doc.	Crcy	Amount in FC
4													
5		CoCode	1000	G/L acct	0000420000	Long Text	Direct labor costs						
6													
7		0000004220	08.01.2004	01 SA	100010062	08.01.2004	001	40				EUR	2.758,34
8		0000004230	08.01.2004	01 SA	100010069	08.01.2004	001	40				EUR	10.647,93
9		0000004220	23.02.2004	02 SA	100010670	23.02.2004	001	40				EUR	2.906,56
10		0000004230	23.02.2004	02 SA	100010677	23.02.2004	001	40				EUR	10.451,40
11		0000004220	01.03.2004	03 SA	100010940	01.03.2004	001	40				EUR	2.831,18
12		0000004230	01.03.2004	03 SA	100010947	01.03.2004	001	40				EUR	11.024,88
13													
14													

That is it! Data copied.

Quick Cut and Paste

Do you want this done quickly? Use **Customize Local Layout Icon** in Standard Tool bar.

Customize Local Layout >> Quick Cut and Paste

In a report just select the portion you want to copy using your mouse + right click and dragging it. Release the mouse after selection. That is it! The portion you selected is copied to clip board. Go to the Word or Excel file and press Cntl + V. Your selection is pasted!.

∞∞

Chapter VII   Customizing SAP Layout

*SAP Layout changes make YOUR SAP FICO **experience a pleasure***

∞

1. Quick Info

You are hovering your mouse on the icons. System tells you what the icon is for? say 'Print', 'Find'. This is the quick info.

Quick info can be enabled or disabled, as you prefer.

Standard Tool Bar: Customize Local Layouts icon >> Options tab, the first sections, **'Quick Info'** section.

Available options are:

- None
- Slow
- Quick

To enable Quick Info you can choose either 'Slow' or 'Quick'

Whenever the cursor moves, say through tab keys, the corresponding Quick Info is displayed.

To disable the Quick Info you find this as too much of distraction, choose 'None'

Click the 'Apply' button.

Additional option is **'On Keyboard Focus Change'**. Enable this to see the Quick Info displayed while the cursor moves from one field to next field, when you use Tab key to navigate.

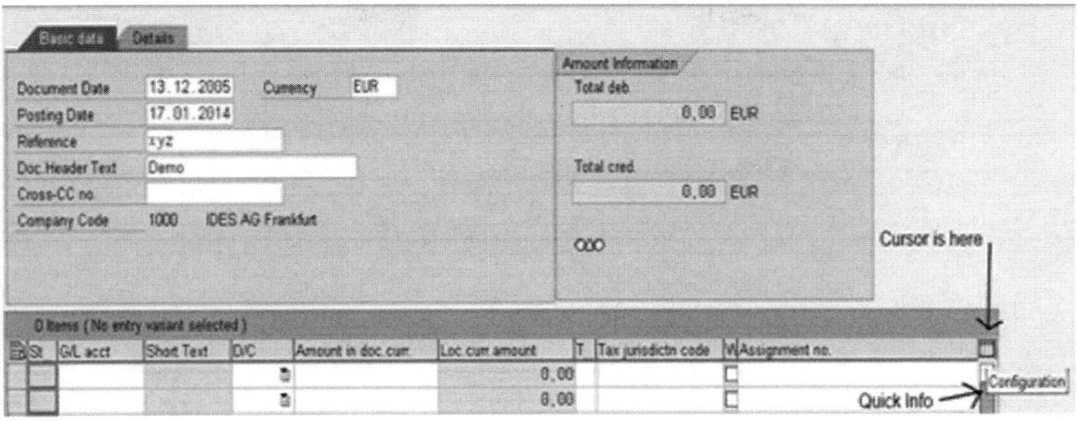

Basic data
Details
Document Date
13.12.2005
Currency
EUR
Posting Date
17.01.2014
Reference
xyz
Doc.Header Text
Demo
Cross-CC no.
Company Code
1000
IDES AG Frankfurt
Amount Information
Total deb.
0,00
EUR
Total cred.
0,00
EUR
Cursor is here
0 Items (No entry variant selected)
St
G/L acct
Short Text
D/C
Amount in doc.curr.
Loc.curr.amount
T
Tax jurisdictn code
W
Assignment no.
0,00
0,00
Configuration
Quick Info

∞

2. Keys in Drop down List

By default, system does not show the 'keys' in 'drop down lists'. 'Keys' are useful for faster data entry.

To enable the Drop down List Keys follow menu path: Standard Tool Bar: Customize Local Layout icon >> 'Expert' tab >> 'Controls' section.

Enable 'Show keys in all Drop down lists' and click 'Apply' button.

When you navigate to a drop-down list, the Quick Info displays the 'Keys'. You can use these keys for choosing the drop down list options during data entry. Example if you want to choose 'Credit' when the cursor is in D/C field type 'H'.

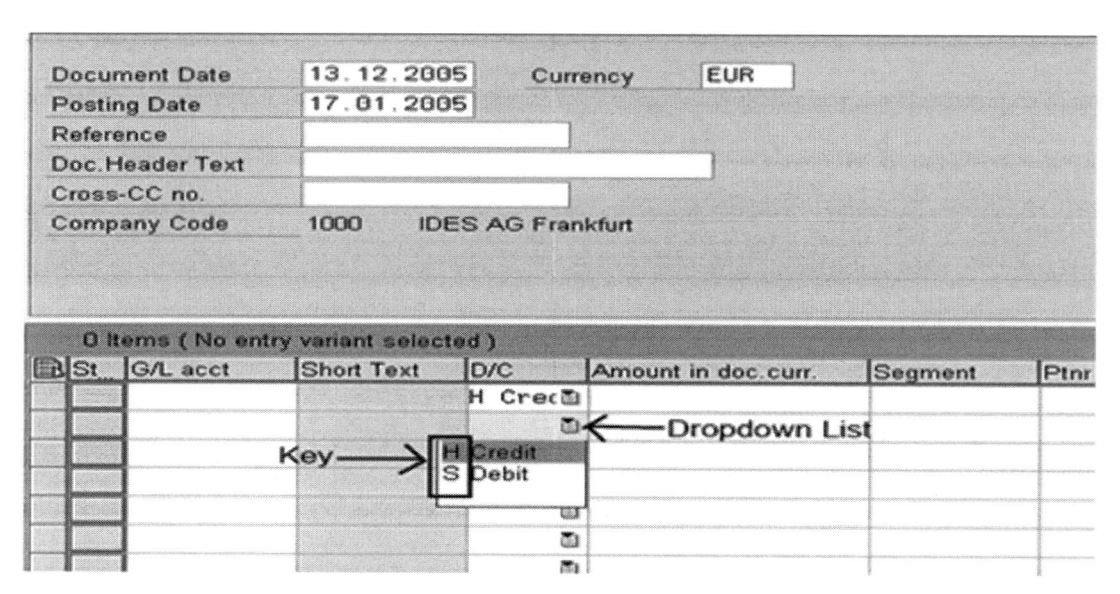

Consider multiple items in the drop down list. You can select 'Sort Items by Key' to see the list sorted by Keys.

3. Changing the Font

While working with SAP have you found the font size of SAP Menu and Menu Bar too small? You can change it as you wish.

Menu path: Standard Tool Bar: Customizing Local Layout Icon >> Font (I18N)

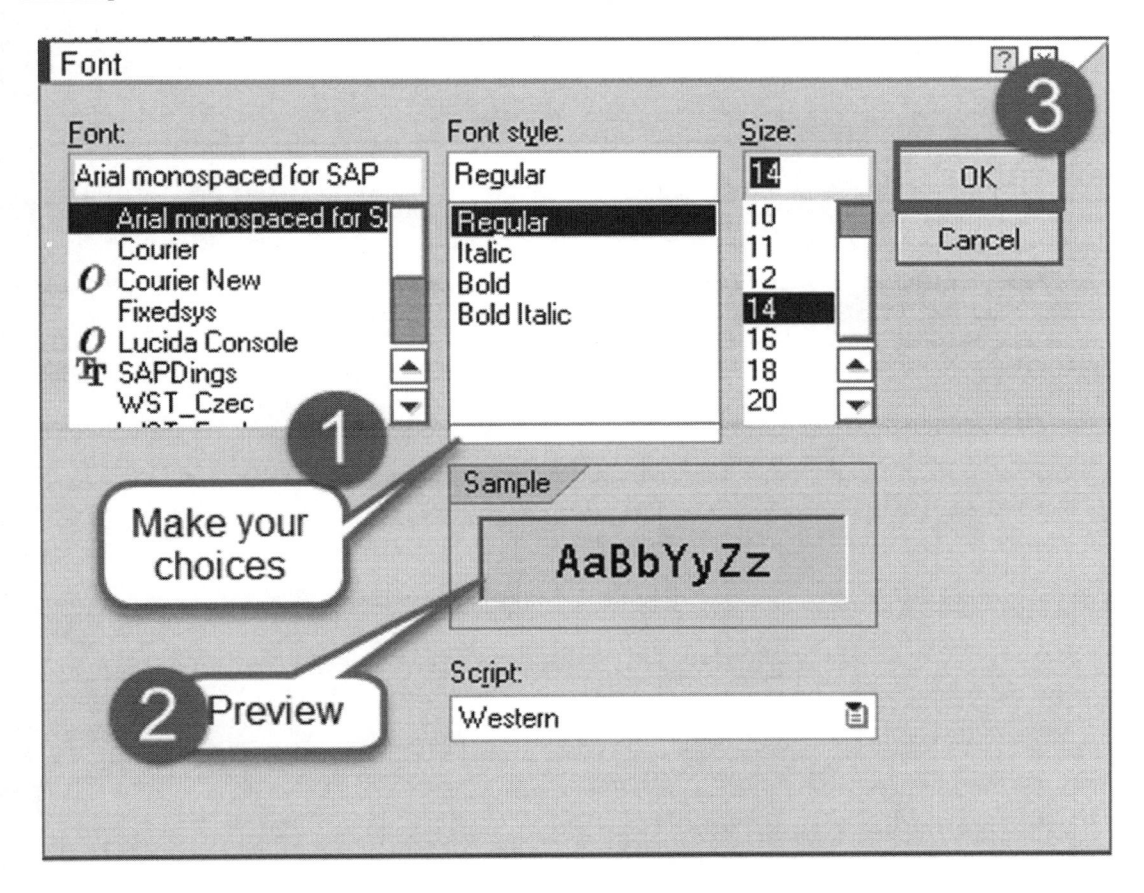

Choose the font, style, size of your choice. When satisfied with the preview click 'ok' button. You may find the icons overlapping. To see them right log off and log on. Now you have the system with the font of your choice.

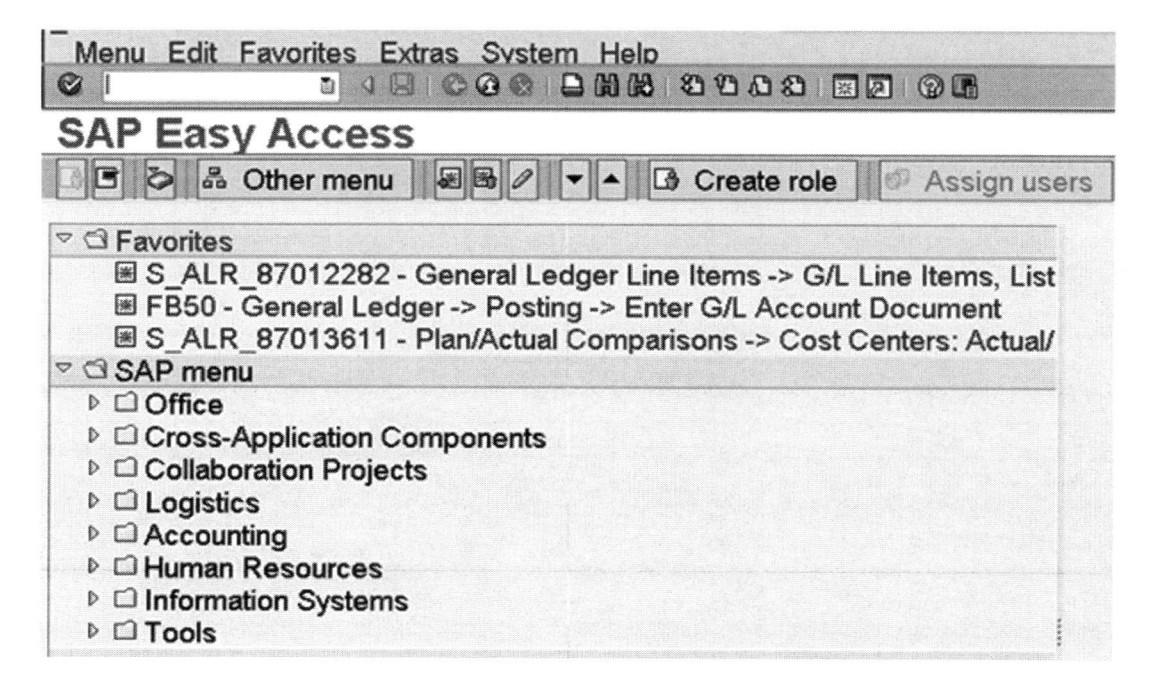

![SAP Easy Access screenshot showing Favorites with S_ALR_87012282 - General Ledger Line Items -> G/L Line Items, List; FB50 - General Ledger -> Posting -> Enter G/L Account Document; S_ALR_87013611 - Plan/Actual Comparisons -> Cost Centers: Actual/; and SAP menu with Office, Cross-Application Components, Collaboration Projects, Logistics, Accounting, Human Resources, Information Systems, Tools]

4. Automatic Tabbing at End of Field

Tip to increase your data entry speed, 'Auto Tabbing' is a handy option!

You are entering data in an input field. Say the required number of characters for the field is 10. Once you enter the 10 characters cursor moves to the next entry field. No need to press 'Tab' key!

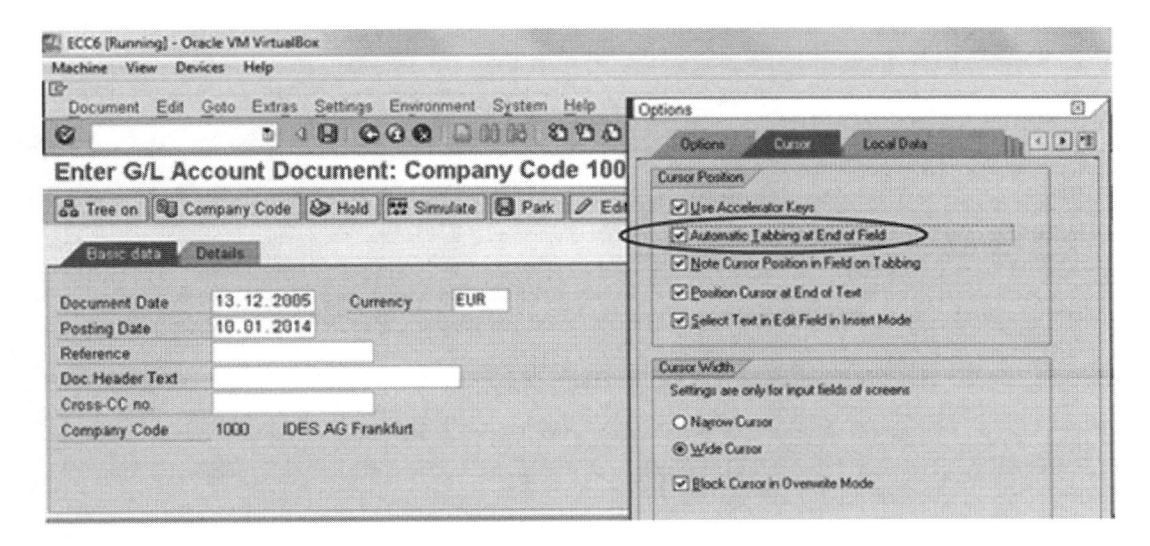

The option is available under 'Customize Local Layout Icon >> Options'

Choose 'Cursor' tab. Under 'Cursor Position', enable 'Automatic Tabbing at End of Field'. Click 'Apply' button.

5. Cursor Behavior While Working in Lists

When you are working in lists, you might come across situation where choosing the entire field makes sense; say the entire text field or the entire values in a column.

This is possible by choosing Standard Tool Bar: Customizing Local Layout Icon >> Options >> Cursor tab >> 'Others' Section >> Deactivate 'Cursor in Lists' check box. Click 'Apply' button.

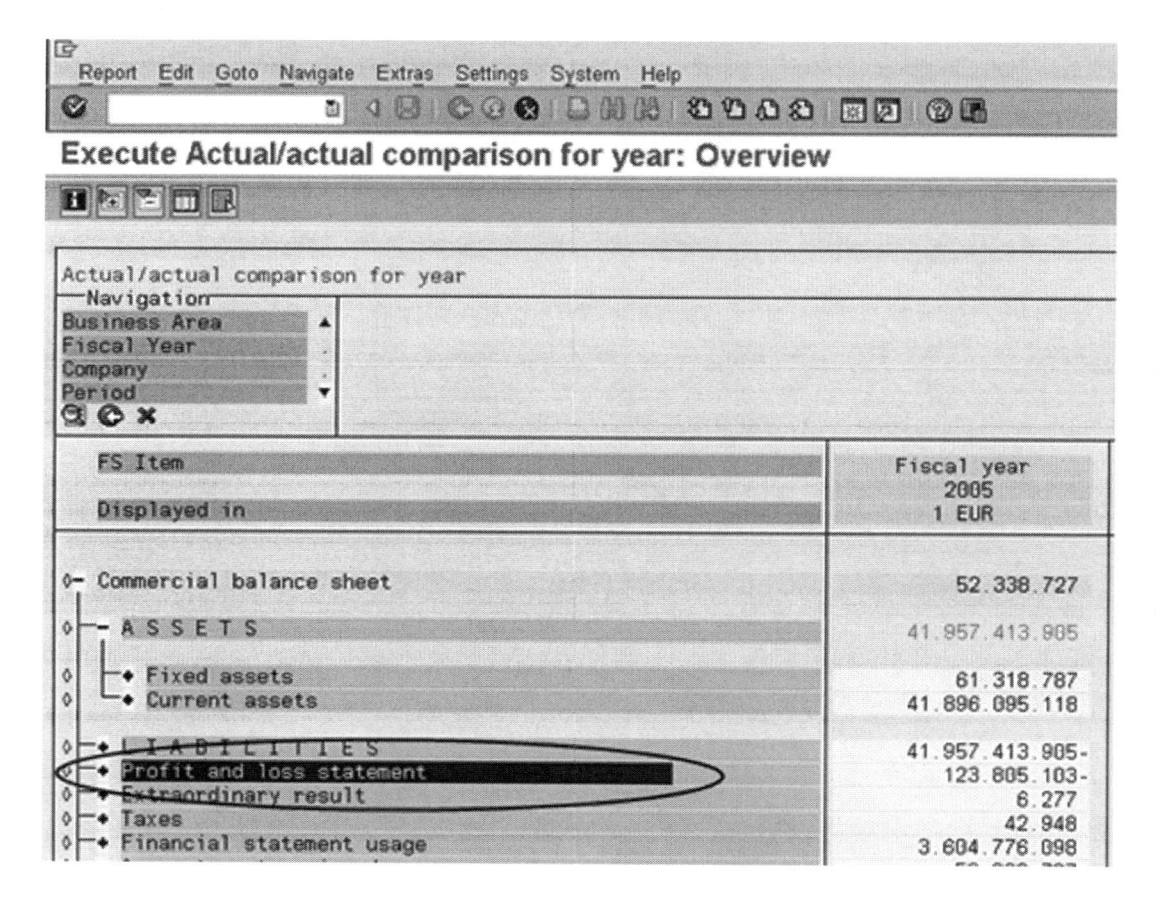

Chapter VIII   Report Parameter Selections

Guide YOU work with Standard Reports

∞

When we run reports in SAP, we need to select parameters. SAP provides useful and friendly options that make selection parameter in SAP so simple and robust.

Let us understand how to use the following user-friendly parameter selection options:

a) Dynamic Selection
b) Multiple Selection
c) Maintain Selection Option

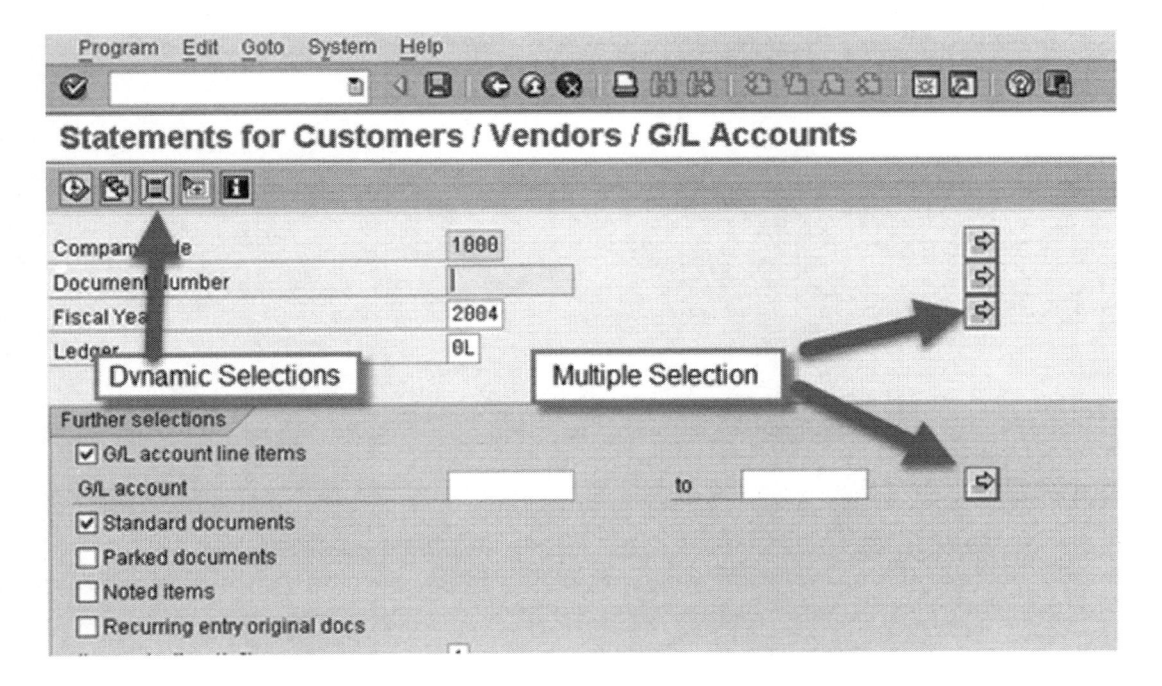

1. Dynamic Selections, Where Used?

Consider running the report **S_ALR_87012332**. Say you want the report for a given period, say Period 5.

The parameter 'Period Selection' option is not apparent in the screen.

Now let us check 'Dynamic Selection' icon.

Click the 'Dynamic Selection' Icon, you can see more report selection options including Period Selection.

Enter Period Selection, say '5' as shown in the next picture to get report data for posting period 5.

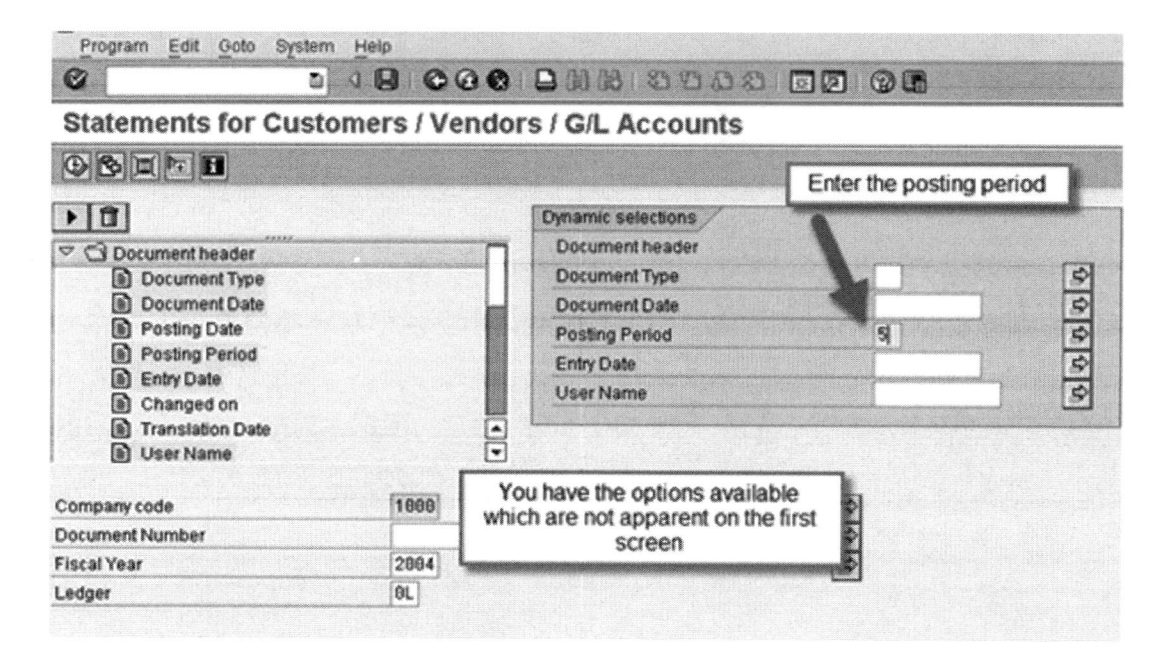

2. Multiple Selection Icons

Let us explore Multiple Selection options for selecting say, GL account codes.

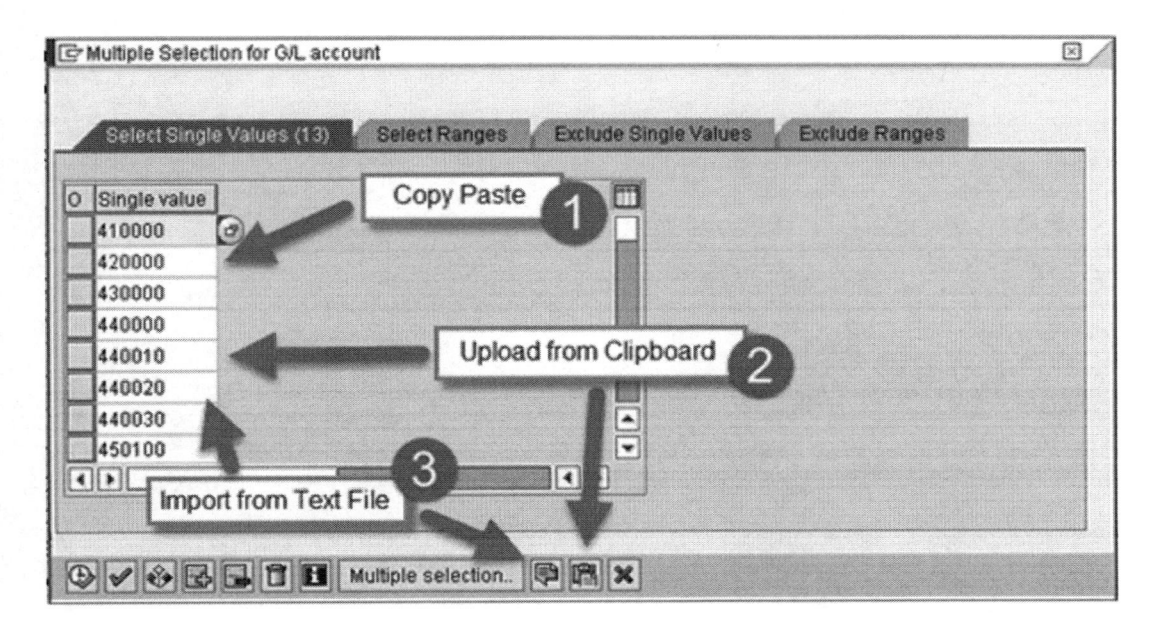

There are **three ways** of doing this.

First Method

You have the GL account codes in an Excel file, for which you want to run the report. You can copy paste them by **Cntl+C & Cntl+V**.

Using this method you can copy paste **8 or fewer** codes only. In other words even if your copied data has say, 13 records, **only 8 of them** will be pasted in this method.

Second Method

Copy the records in the Excel file by **Cntl+C** and then click '**Upload from Clipboard**' icon as marked '2' in the picture. **All the records**, say 13 records you have, will be copied.

80 SAP FICO BEGINNER'S HANDBOOK

Third Method

By selecting **'Import from Text File'**, marked 3 in the picture system will prompt for the selection of the text file and once the text file is selected, **all the records**, even when exceeding 8, will be copied.

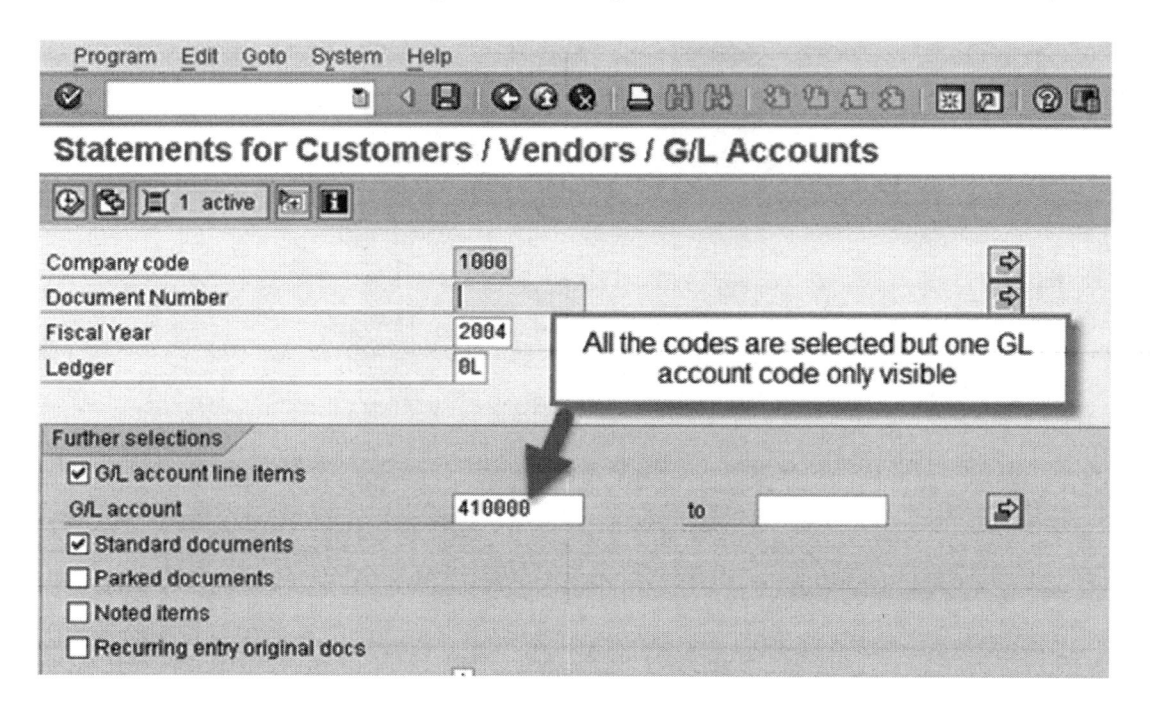

[screenshot: Statements for Customers / Vendors / G/L Accounts selection screen showing Company code 1000, Fiscal Year 2004, Ledger 0L, G/L account 410000, with annotation "All the codes are selected but one GL account code only visible"]

Once copied click **'Execute'** icon or press **F8** to get the data in the report selection screen. You will see **only one record visible** here. However, **system has taken all your records** as copied and the report generated will produce you the results for GL account codes of say, 13 records as copied by you.

∞

3. Dynamic Selection icon

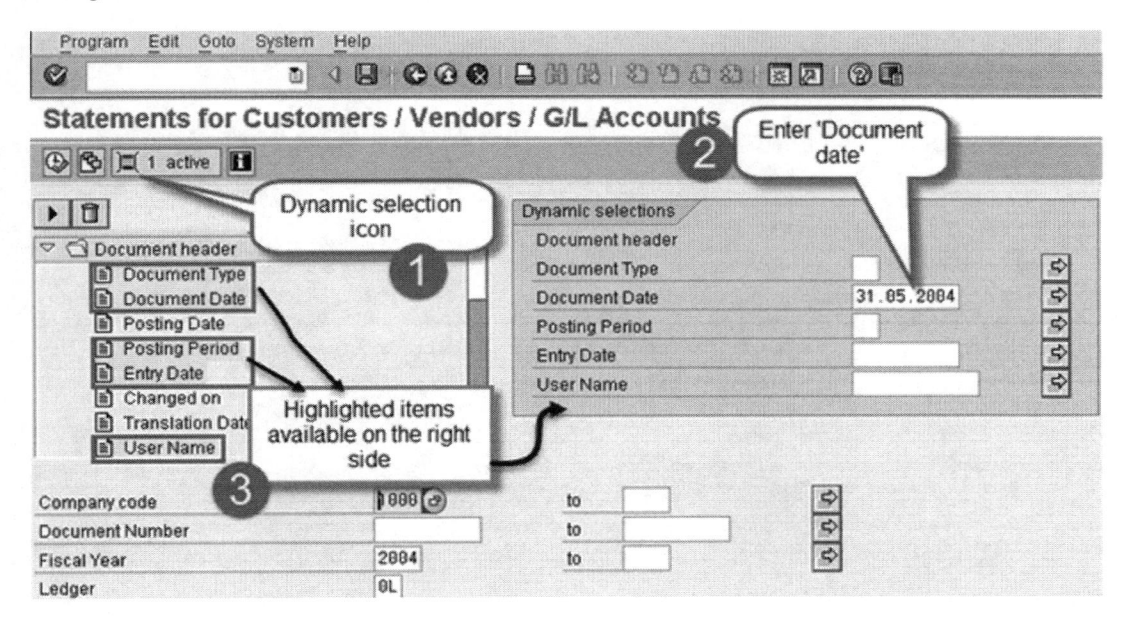

We briefly saw the use of Dynamic Selection Icon in the last section. This is a very useful but often not fully used icon that needs little more attention!

When you run a report say S_ALR_87012332, you want the report for 31st May 2004. There is no option in the Selection screen to choose the Document date.

1. Now click Dynamic Selection icon.

2. Enter Document date as shown and run the report to get data you wanted.

3. The highlighted items in the left window are available on the right side for you to make choices. If you want say 'Changed on' to the right side double click the item.

4. Maintain Selection Options Icon and its Use

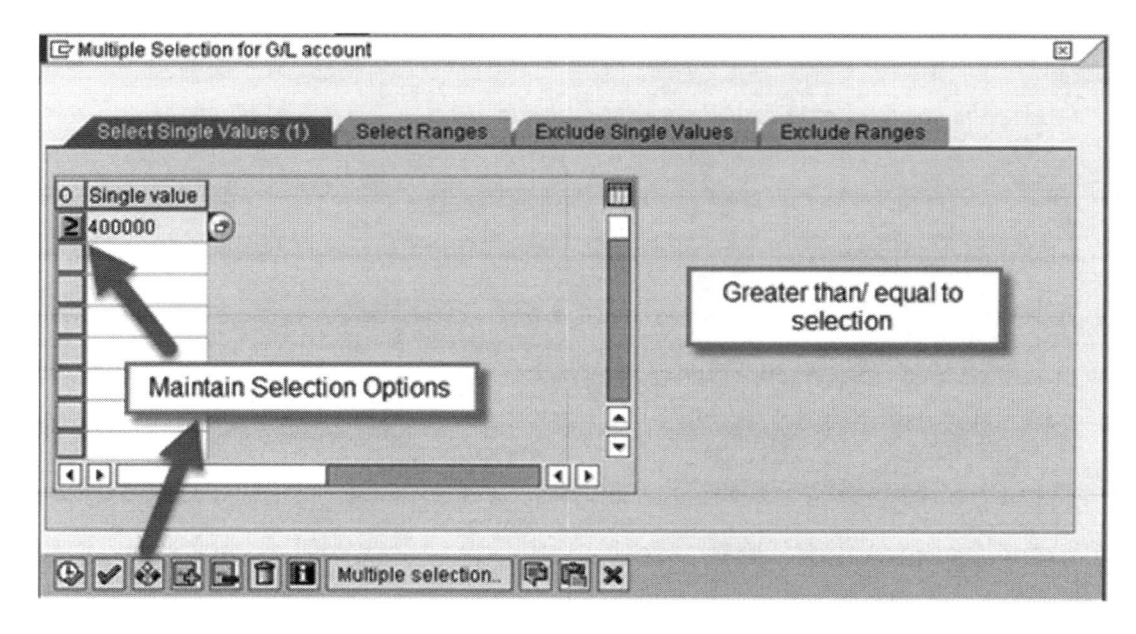

You want to run a report for all GL account codes **greater than OR equal to**, say 400000. Choose '**Maintain Selection Options**' and select 'Greater than /equal to' option.

Enter the GL account code 400000. Press **F8** and run the report to get all of GL account codes of 400000 and greater!

Other options available in Maintain Selection Options are:

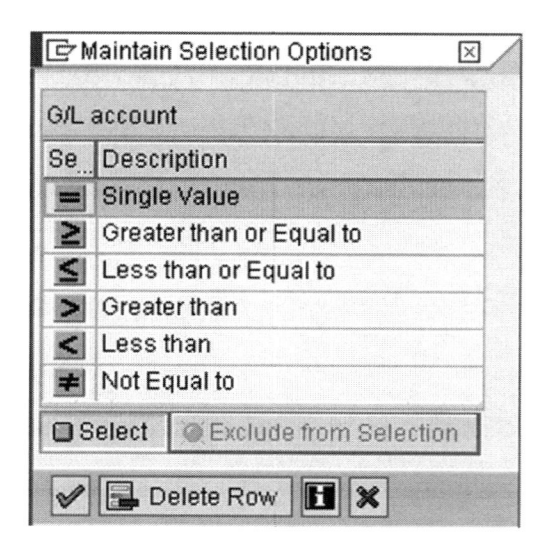

- Single Value
- Less than or Equal to
- Greater than
- Less than
- Not Equal to

Selection Variant

Selection Variant in SAP is one of the productivity enhancement tools that makes SAP User life pleasant.

Consider we need to run a report, GL Account Statements, TCode-S_ALR_87012332 with following parameters:

- Company code: **1000**
- Fiscal year: **2004**
- Document number '**no selection**'
- Ledger: **0l**
- GL Account: **430000**, Direct Labor Cost

Running the report with above selections gives us the report we wanted.

Why Selection Variant?

What are the benefits of defining and using Selection Variant, let us have a look. Say,

> We want to run the report with all the above parameters except the GL code. GL account code to be entered dynamically; i.e., at the time of running the report.
>
> We do not want to be distracted with many options that are not relevant to our purpose and no requirement for any selection.
>
> We do not want the field Company Code editable while running the report.
>
> We can give the task of running the report to our colleagues with minimum instruction.

The above are precisely the benefits of defining and using selection variant.

Defining Selection Variant

Let us understand how to proceed in 5 steps.

SAP FICO BEGINNER'S HANDBOOK 85

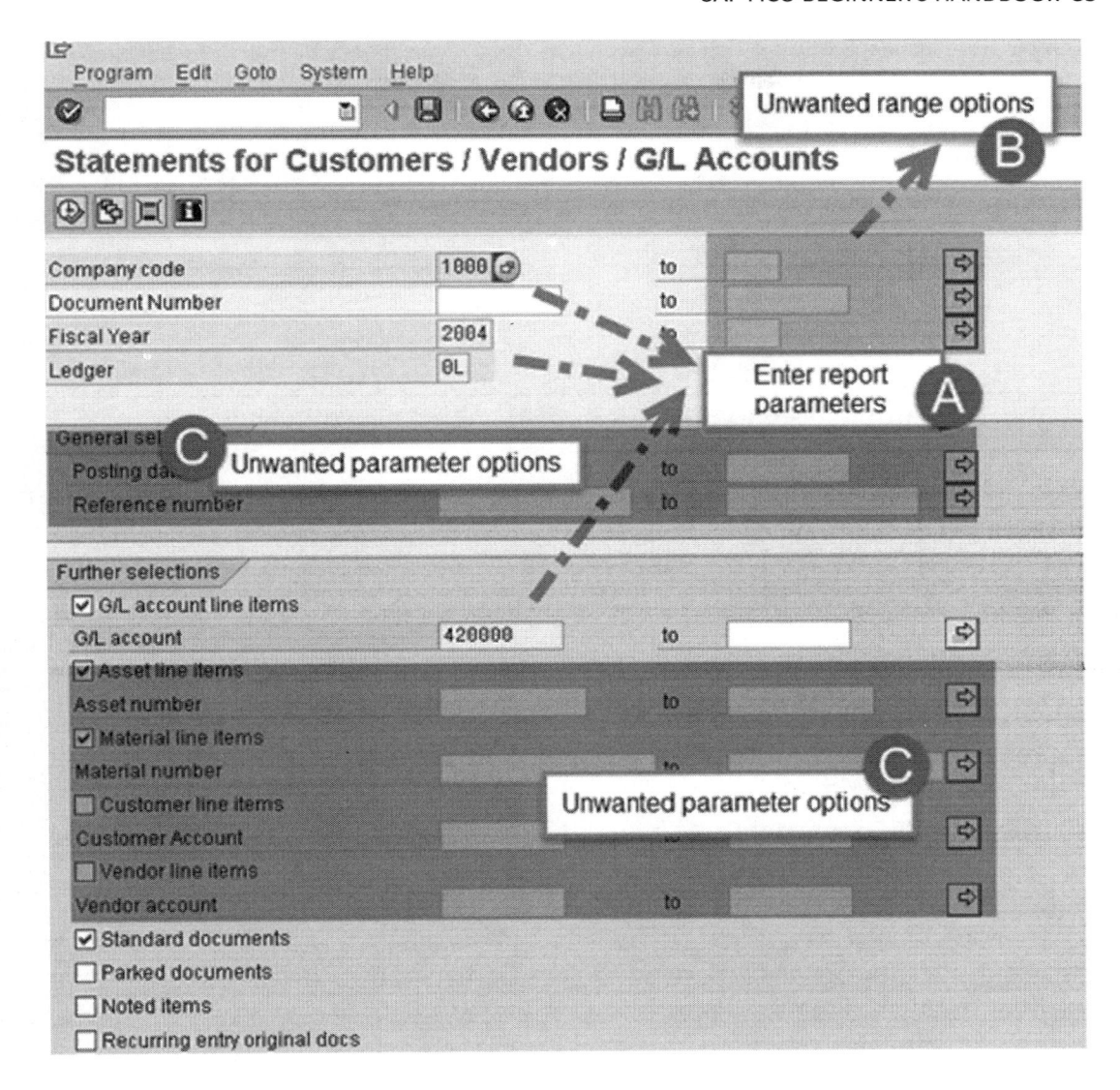

[Screenshot: Statements for Customers / Vendors / G/L Accounts selection screen with annotations — A: Enter report parameters; B: Unwanted range options; C: Unwanted parameter options]

Step 1

Enter the following parameters in the cells marked '**A**'

- Company code **1000**
- Fiscal year **2004**
- Document number **'no selection'**
- Ledger **0l**
- GL Account **430000**

Step 2

Identify 'Range Selection' (marked '**B**') that we do not want:

- Company code
- Fiscal Year
- Ledger

Step 3

Identify the parameter entry cells that we do not need, highlighted under '**C**':

- Posting date
- Reference number
- Asset Line items
- Material Line items
- Customer Line items
- Vendor Line items

Step 4

Click 'Save' icon in the main tool bar next to command window OR

Follow menu path **Go to >> Variants >> Save as Variant** OR

Press Cntl + S in the keyboard, to go to Variant Attributes Screen.

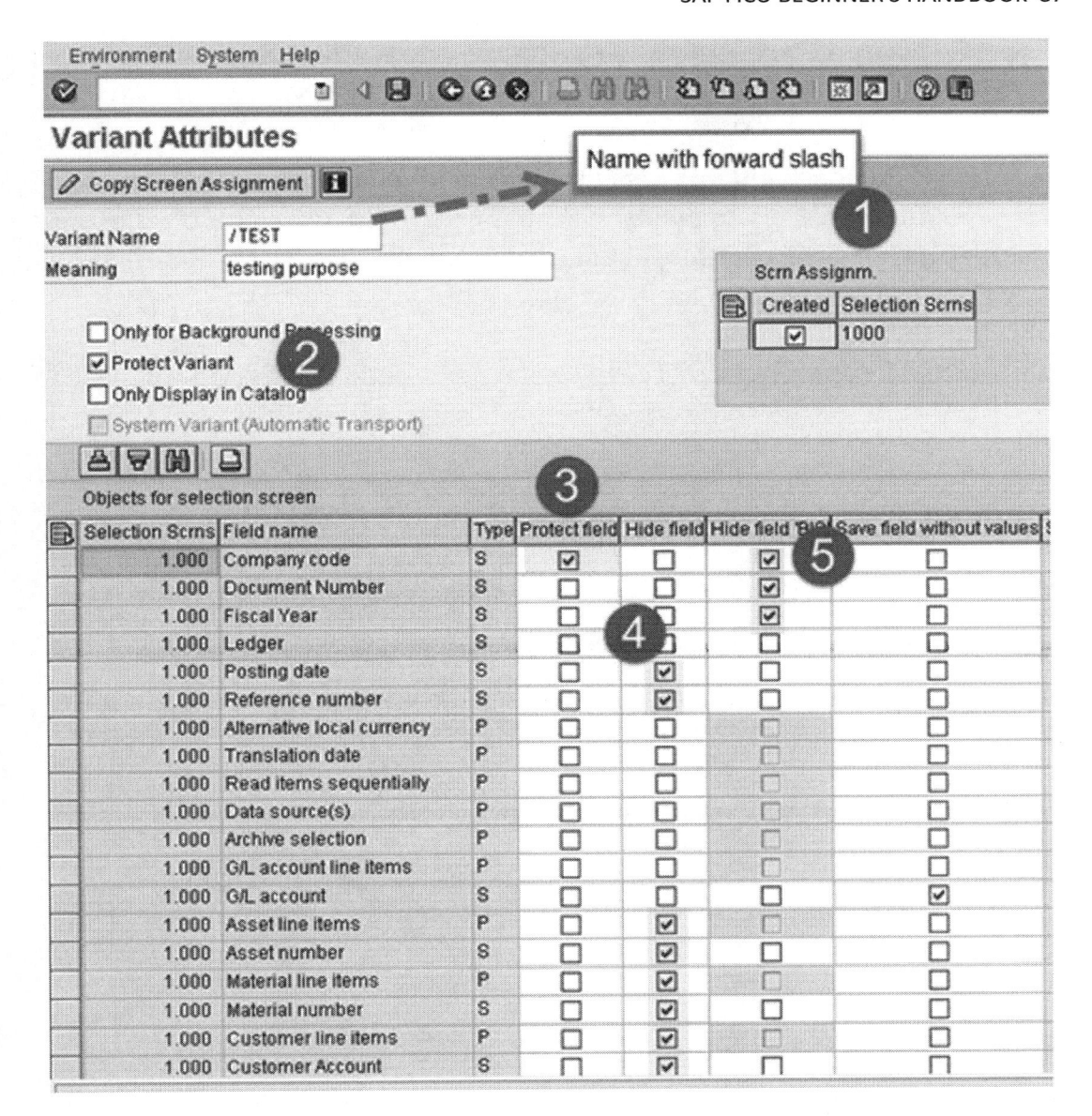

Step 5

Enter name with forward slash. Forward slash is required to make this variant available to other SAP users.

- Check '**Protect Variant**'. Only you can edit the variant. Other users cannot edit your variant
- Check '**Protect Field**' against Company Code. This field will not be editable during program running using the selection variant

- Check **'Hide Field'** against Posting Date, Reference Number and other highlighted lines. These fields will not appear while running the program, thus avoiding unwanted distractions
- Check **'Hide Field BIS'** against Company Code, Document Number and Fiscal Year. This prevents system showing 'Range Options' and these fields will have only single value entry options
- Now click **'Save'**. Variant '/test' is saved

You may have a question. What is the use of defining a variant that can be used by others?

Such a variant enables you to request your colleague to run the report using the variant you defined, thus helps increasing your productivity.

Running the Report using the Selection Variant

Enter TCode S_ALR_87012332 in the command window and press 'Enter'

Choose **'Select Variant'** icon in the application tool bar OR follow menu path 'Go To >> Variants >> Get Variant'

Window with many Selection Variants pops up. Choose '/test' variant from the pop up list.

Press 'Enter'.

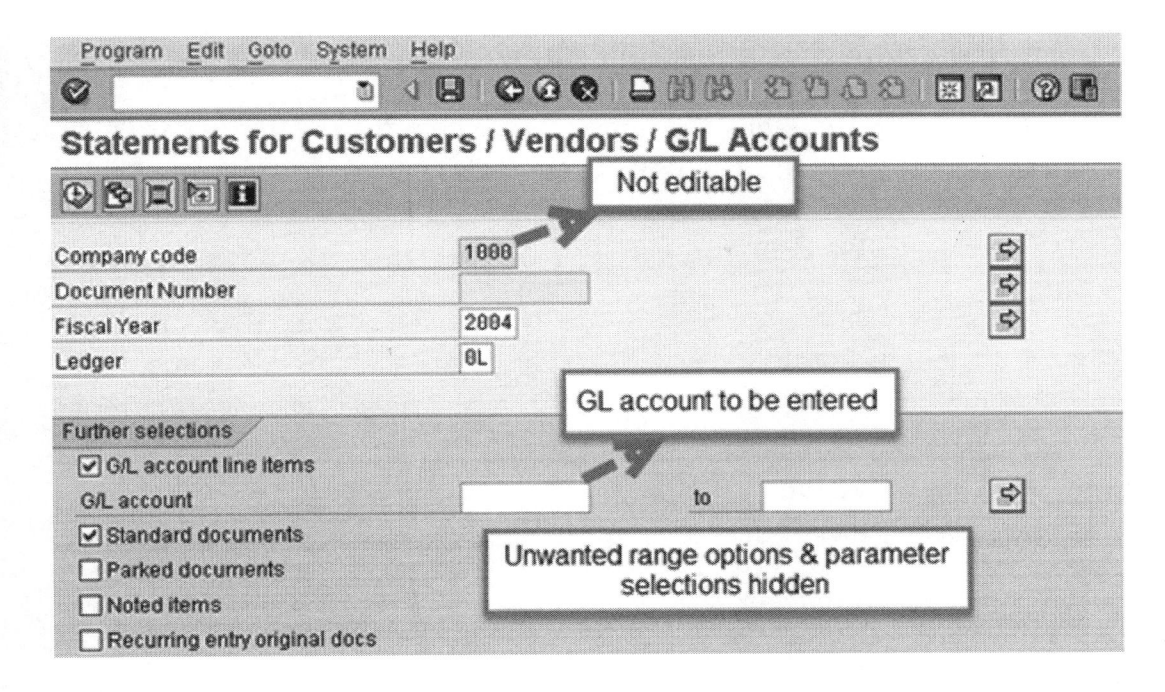

Statements for Customers / Vendors / G/L Accounts

(Screen shows selection screen with the following fields and annotations:)

- Company code: 1000 — **Not editable**
- Document Number:
- Fiscal Year: 2004
- Ledger: 0L
- **GL account to be entered**

Further selections
- ☑ G/L account line items
- G/L account ____ to ____
- ☑ Standard documents
- ☐ Parked documents
- ☐ Noted items
- ☐ Recurring entry original docs

Unwanted range options & parameter selections hidden

We get the 'Selection Screen' the way we wanted!

<u>While using the selection variant</u> as above you want the hidden fields to appear. This is possible. Follow menu path **Edit >> All Selections**. Again, if you want those fields to be hidden, then follow the menu path **Edit >> Chosen Selections**.

Dynamic Selection of Date Field

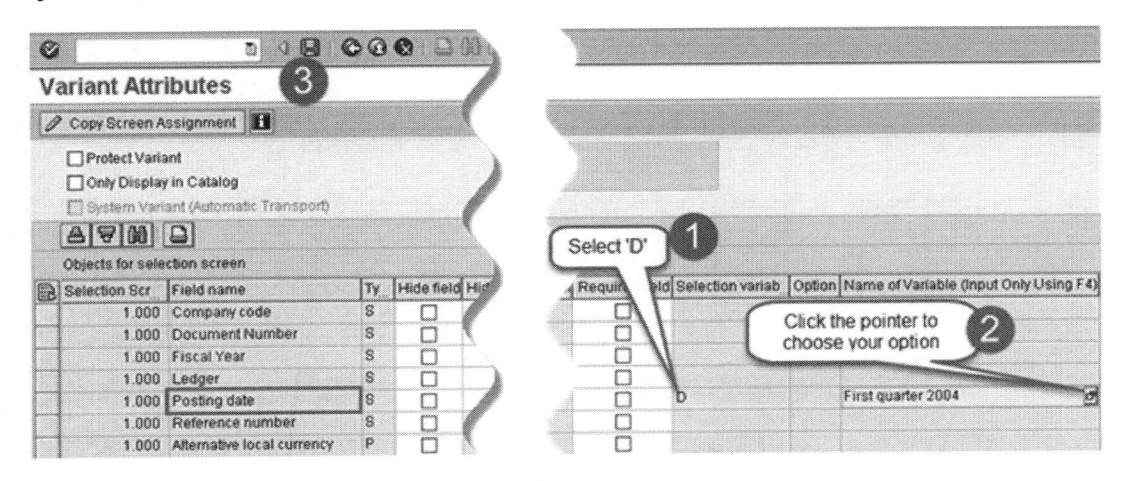

(Screen shows Variant Attributes with annotations:)

- ❸ Variant Attributes
- ☐ Protect Variant
- ☐ Only Display in Catalog
- ☐ System Variant (Automatic Transport)

Objects for selection screen:

Selection Scr	Field name	Ty	Hide field	...	Requi...	...ld	Selection variab	Option	Name of Variable (Input Only Using F4)
1.000	Company code	S	☐		☐				
1.000	Document Number	S	☐		☐				
1.000	Fiscal Year	S	☐		☐				
1.000	Ledger	S	☐		☐				
1.000	Posting date	S	☐		☐		D		First quarter 2004
1.000	Reference number	S	☐		☐				
1.000	Alternative local currency	P	☐		☐				

❶ **Select 'D'**

❷ **Click the pointer to choose your option**

Let us choose the same report TCode **S_ALR_87012332**.

Let us start over creating another variant to understand this option. Let us define selection variant for 'Posting Date'.

1. Select 'D' under the column **Selection Variable**, against row **Posting Date**.

2. Select, say **'First Quarter ????'** option by clicking the pointer under column **'Name of the Variable'**, against **'Posting Date'** row.

Let us look at available options:

- Current Date
- From month start to today
- Current date +/- ??? days
- current date +/- ??? work days
- First day of current month
- nth working day of current month
- First day of next month
- First day of previous month
- Last day of previous month
- Last Day of the Current Month
- **First quarter ????**
- Second quarter ????
- Third quarter ????
- Fourth quarter ????
- Current date - xxx,current date + yyy
- Date - xxx, Date + yyy (work days)
- Previous month
- Current period
- (Beginning of mth-xx months, end of mth+yy months)

'????' indicate the year field. When you choose say 'First Quarter' system prompts you to enter the year. I have chosen 2004.

3. Click 'Save' button to save the variant.

Now use the variant defined as above to populate in one-step all the report parameters you wanted including the *date defined dynamically*.

Company code	1000	to	
Document Number		to	
Fiscal Year	2004	to	
Ledger	0L		

General selections

Posting date	01.01.2004	to	31.03.2004
Reference number		to	

First quarter as defined in the variant

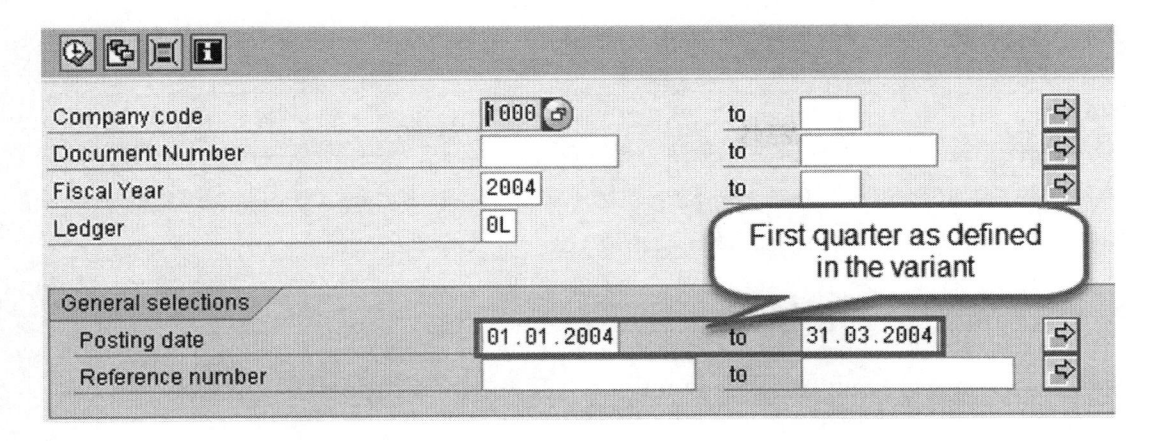

Consider the various options available to define the date, it empowers you like say '**From month start today**', the correct date is selected month after month so you can run a report quickly to get report for say, Month to Date.

∞

6. Report Layout Changes

You are running a General Ledger Report. SAP generates the report in the standard format. You take a sip of coffee and start making changes to the report. Yes, now you have the information you wanted, in the way you wanted! Are you tired of making the changes every time you run the report?

No worries, we have SAP Tips, Report Layout Changes that hold the key!

Let us see how we can tell SAP what you need from a report!

SAP Report Layout Changes

Report layout changes, saved once, available at a click away! New layout is available even to your team.

Let us consider the report -GL Line Items, List for Printing

Type in the command line S_ALR_87012282 and hit 'Enter'

Menu path: Accounting >> Financial Accounting >> General Ledger >> Information System >> General Ledger Reports >> Line Items >> General Ledger Line Items >> GL Line Items, List for Printing

Choose your parameters, Chart of Account, GL Account, Company Code

Hit F8 to get your report:

SAP FICO BEGINNER'S HANDBOOK 93

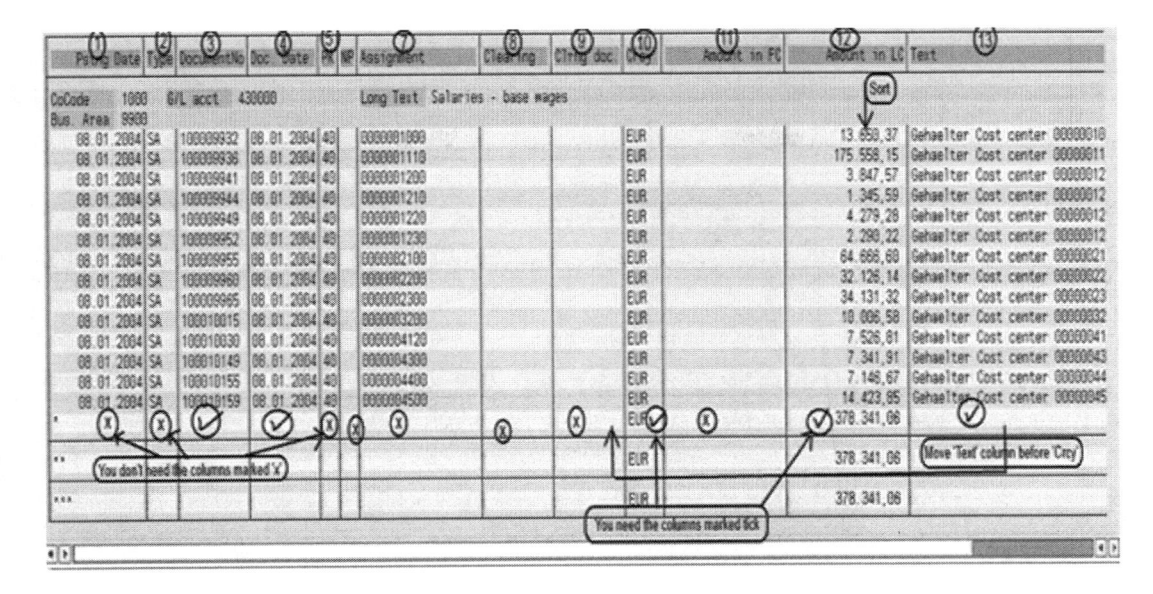

You finally want the report like the one below:

- from a 13 column to 5 columns you need most of the times,
- the amount column sorted, largest amount to smallest,
- 'Text' column to appear before 'Currency'

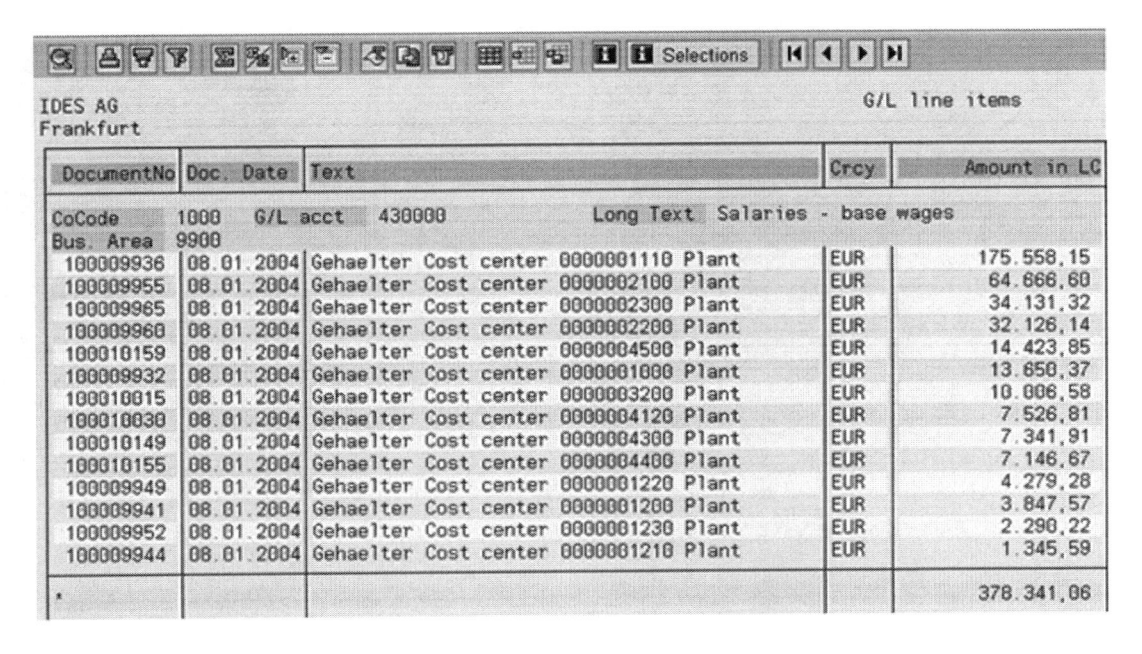

Let us see how you can get the report layout all the time, by just doing once and saving the layout.

94 SAP FICO BEGINNER'S HANDBOOK

Cntl + F8 or 'Change Layout' icon, clicking this icon takes you to 'Change Layout' screen. You can see two boxes; first one lists the Report Column headings, Position, Length and Summation options.

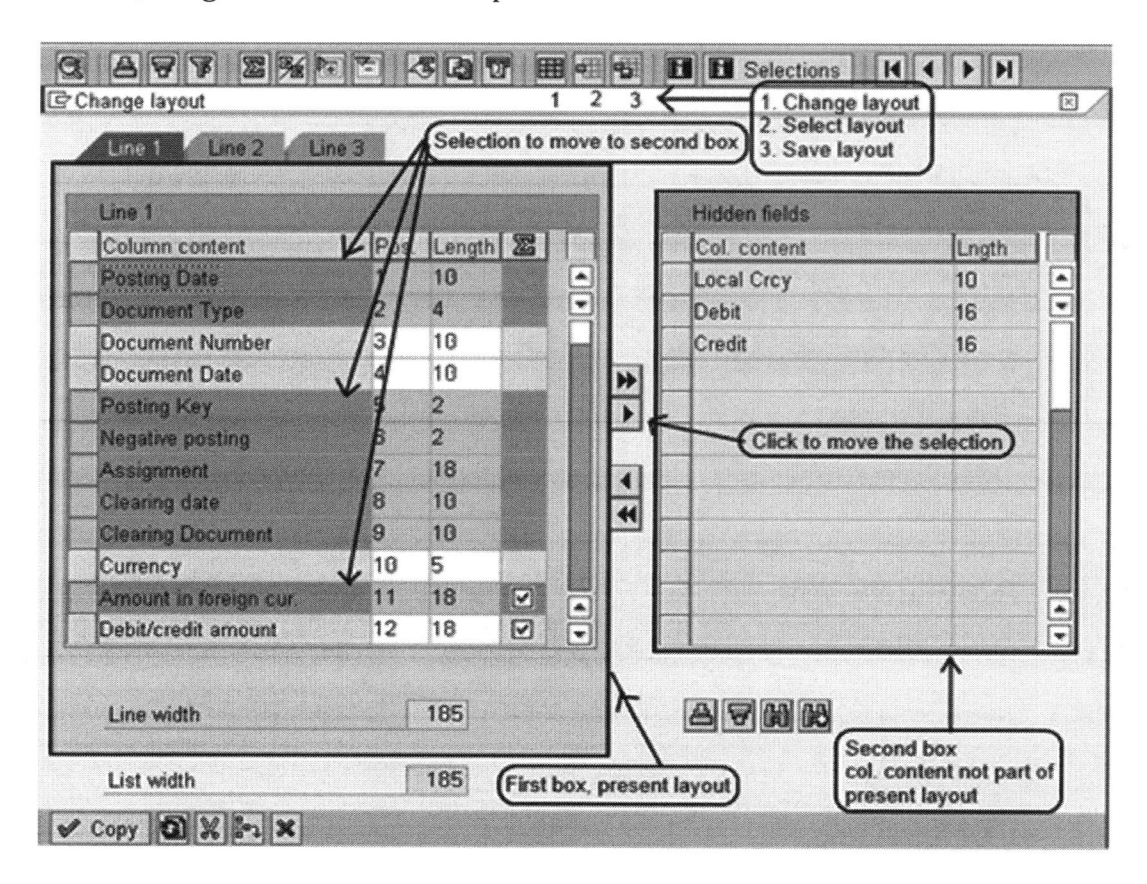

Select from the list the columns you do not need and move them to the second box. To change the order of the columns, use cut and paste options - select 'Text' column content, click 'Cut', select 'Currency' column content, click 'Paste'. Now Text column is moved to the desired place. Click 'Copy', you can see the results of the changes you made in the Change Layout Screen.

Select the column you want the data to be sorted. Click 'Sort' icon or hit 'Cntl + +Shift+F4'. Now the report is ready the way you wanted!

Save Layout

To save the layout, hit Cntl+F10 or click 'Save Layout' icon. Give the layout a name and description. To make the layout available to everyone give the name starting with forward slash.

Layout name starting with a forward slash, makes the layout design as default design, which will be available to all the users.

Just in case you want to keep the layout design for yourself, then you need to save the layout without the forward slash.

Using Saved Layout

How to get the result every time you run the report:

When you run the Report next time, getting the saved layout is simple by Cntl+F9, or click Select Layout Icon, choose your saved layout design. That is it!. You got the report as you designed.

∞

7. Report Parameter by Default

SAP Tricks that can reduce your data entry for SAP Controlling report generation; you need to **tell SAP only once** what your preferences are. These preferences will be entered as default values whenever you run the report. *No worries*, in case you need a different selection, you can always change these values as and when you need a different report.

Cost Element Accounting Reports

T Code: **rpa0**

Menu path is Accounting >> Controlling >> Cost Element Accounting >> Information System >> User Settings

Basic Data *tab* for the choices - Controlling Area & Company Code

Enter your Controlling Area & the Company Code, which you would most often required to run the reports.

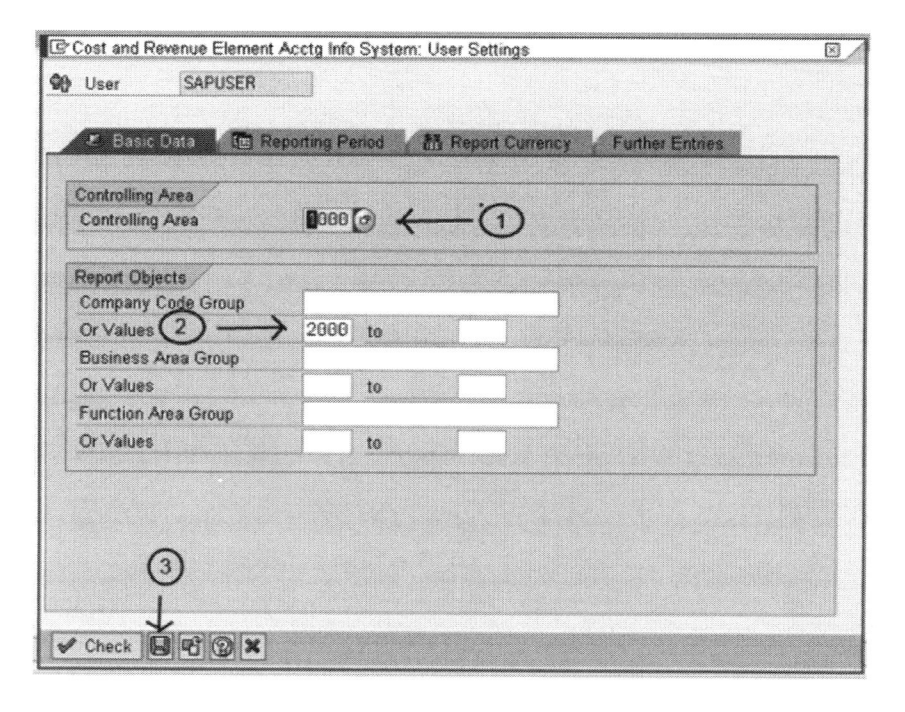

Reporting Period tab for the choices -

- *Fiscal Year*

- *Current year*
- *Previous year*
- *Other*

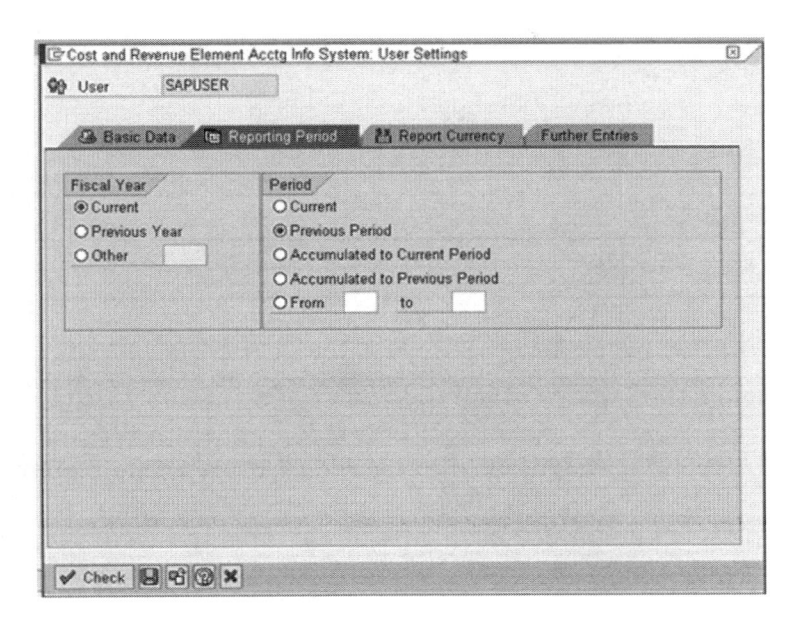

My choice is Current year as often the current year analysis is what report requirement most of the time. You can make your choice.

Second choice is for *Period*

Choices are
- Current period
- Previous period
- Accumulated to Current Period
- Accumulated to Previous period
- From & To

If you run the reports for the Previous period most times you can make this choice OR make your choice as required in your case.

Make these choices once and save it. Whenever you run your Cost Element reports, you will find the choices made here already entered. You have the option to run the report or over ride the values to suit your report requirements.

Other choices are *Report Currency* tab & *Further Entries* tab.

Cost Center Accounting Reports

T Code: **rpc0**

Menu path: Accounting >> Controlling >> Cost Center Accounting >> Information System >> User Settings

Basic Data for the choices -

- *Controlling Area*
- *Cost Center Group or Values*
- *Activity Type Group or Values*
- *Statistical Group or Values*
- *Cost Element Group or Values*

Make your choices for these values based on your report requirements.

Planning Period & Reporting Period tabs for choosing Fiscal Year & Period of your choice.

Report Currency & Further Entries tabs for more options.

Internal Orders Reports

T Code: **rpo0**

Menu path: *Accounting >> Controlling >> Internal Orders >> Information System >> User Settings*

Basic Data tab for choosing

- *Controlling Area*
- *Order Group or Values,*
- *Cost Element Group or Values*

Use Planning Period and Reporting Period tabs for your choices on Fiscal year & Period.

Use 'Report Currency' and 'Further Entries' tabs for more choices.

∞∞

Chapter IX   List Functions

*Experience **authority** learning LIST FUNCTIONS*

∞

In this chapter, we will see how to apply the powerful list functions - sort, filter and subtotal.

1. Sort Order - Simple & Multi Level

<u>Data used</u>: TCode FBL3N - Display/Change Line Items

Simple Sort on single column: This can be achieved by selecting the column to be sorted and 'Edit >> Sort in Ascending order or Descending order' as required.

To have **Multi Level Sort** we need to follow as below:

1. Make sure **NO** column in the list is selected.

2. Choose 'Edit >> Sort in Ascending Order OR Sort in Descending Order' or Click the 'sort' icon.

3. Dialog box for defining sort conditions opens.

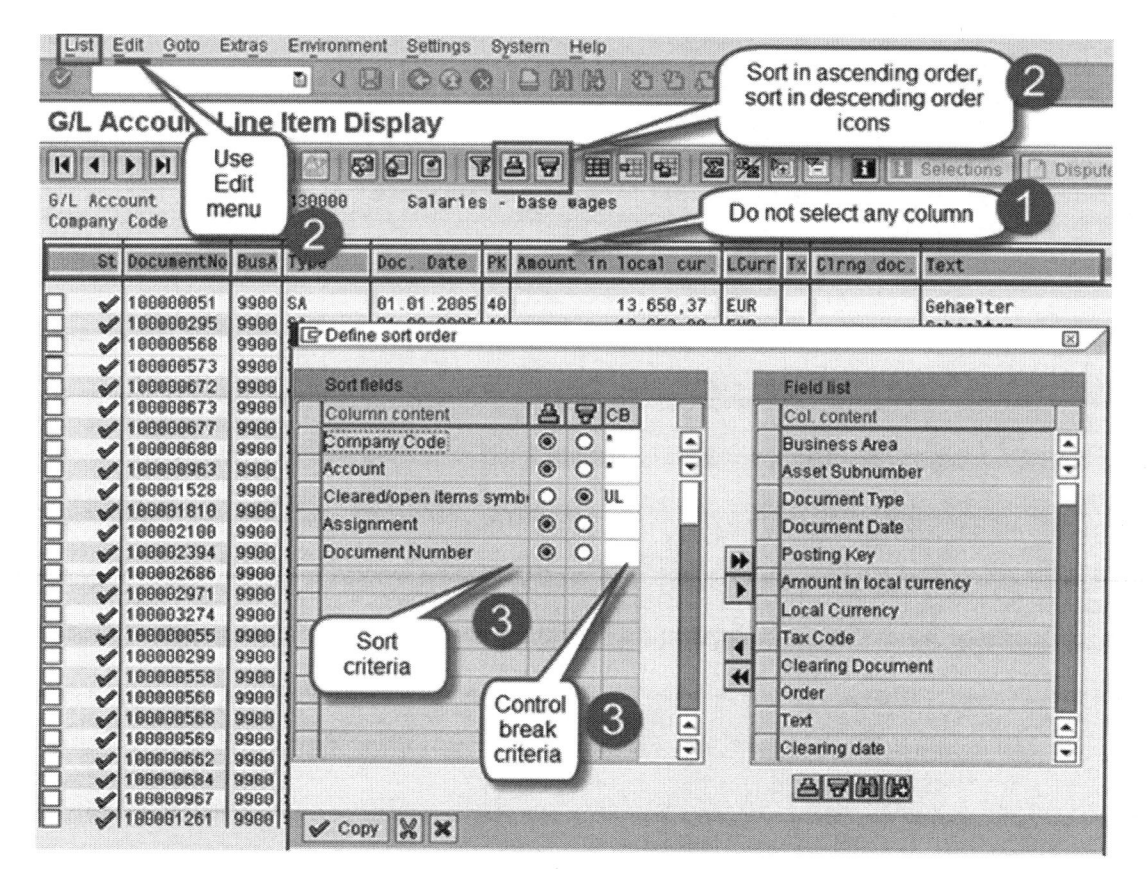

In the picture, we have defined criteria:

1. Ascending order on Company code
2. Ascending order on GL account
3. Descending order on Cleared/Open symbol
4. Ascending order on Assignment
5. Ascending order on Document Number

Control Break criteria - Meaning of '*' & 'UL'

Asterisk mark indicate 'Page feed including underline'

UL indicate 'Under Line', no page break.

In the given example Company Code and GL account have 'asterisk' marks as Control Break criteria.

That means, List have page breaks for Company Code and GL account combination.

Clear/ Open Item symbol has 'UL' as the Control Break criteria. This means the list will have separate sections with underline for Open Items and Cleared Items.

Assignment and Document marked as ascending order means the list will be sorted <u>first</u> on Assignment and <u>within Assignment sorted list</u> on Document number.

If you have noticed, Assignment is not visible in the list. However, <u>system can sort on this hidden column</u> also.

∞

2. Filter - Multi Level

Data used: TCode FBL3N - Display/Change Line Items

1. Make sure **NO** column in the list is selected.

2. Choose 'Edit >> Set Filter' OR Click the 'Set Filter' icon.

3. Dialog box for defining 'Filter Conditions' opens. On the right side of the dialog box contains all field items. Select the item and move them to the left side window of the dialog box.

4. Press 'Enter' or click Copy.

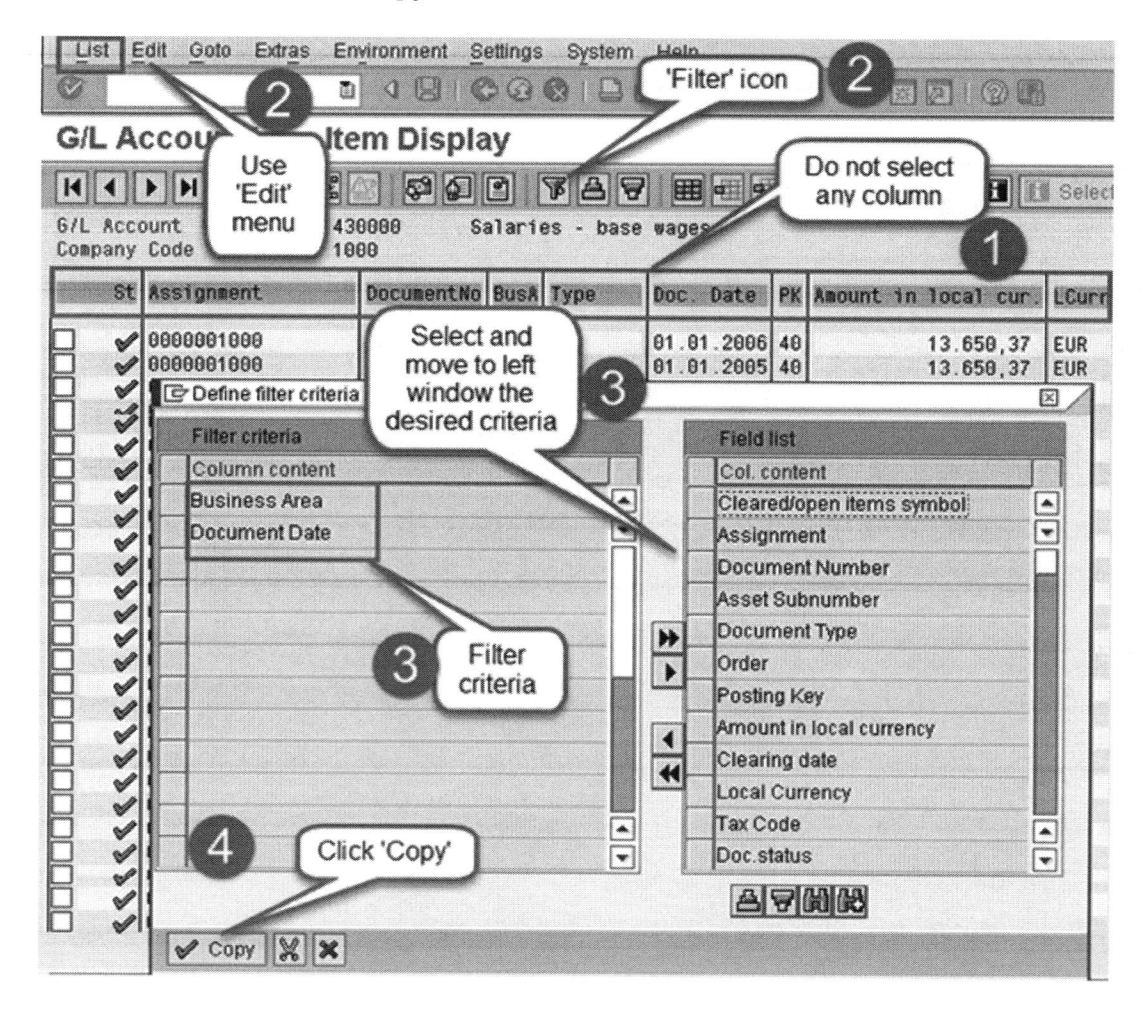

Dialog box for setting filter criteria opens.

SAP FICO BEGINNER'S HANDBOOK 103

a) Define the filter criteria limits.

b) You can define complex limits choosing 'Multiple Selections' icon.

Press 'Enter' to get the filtered list.

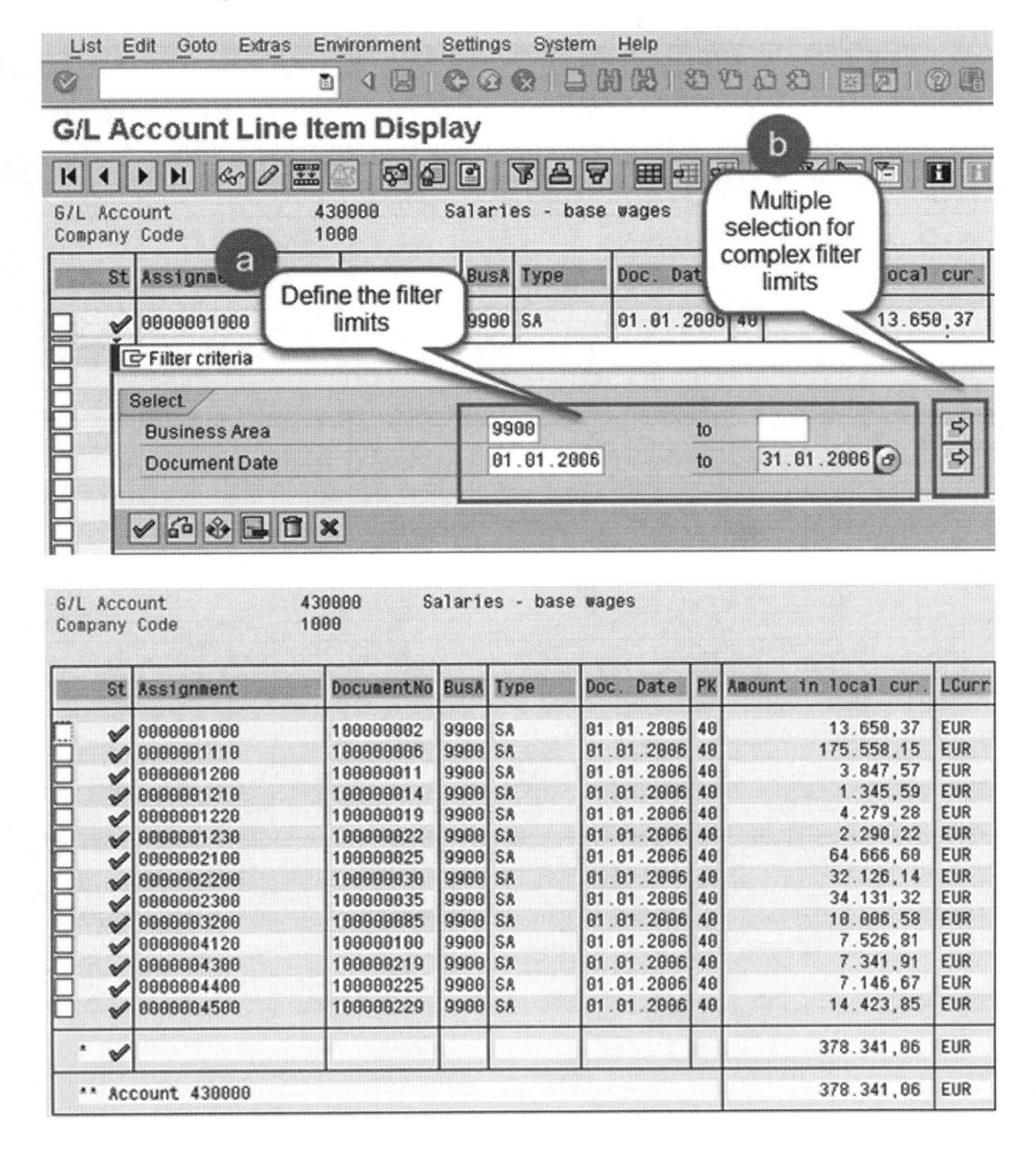

3. Subtotal - Simple and Multilevel

Important: To use subtotal function at least one column 'Total' should be active.

1. Click the 'Subtotal' icon or Edit >> Subtotal

2. Select the fields for which you want to apply 'Subtotal'.

3. Click the arrow pointing to the left to move the selected field to left window.

4. Enable the check box against the fields under the column 'subtotal'.

5. Press 'Enter' or click 'Copy'.

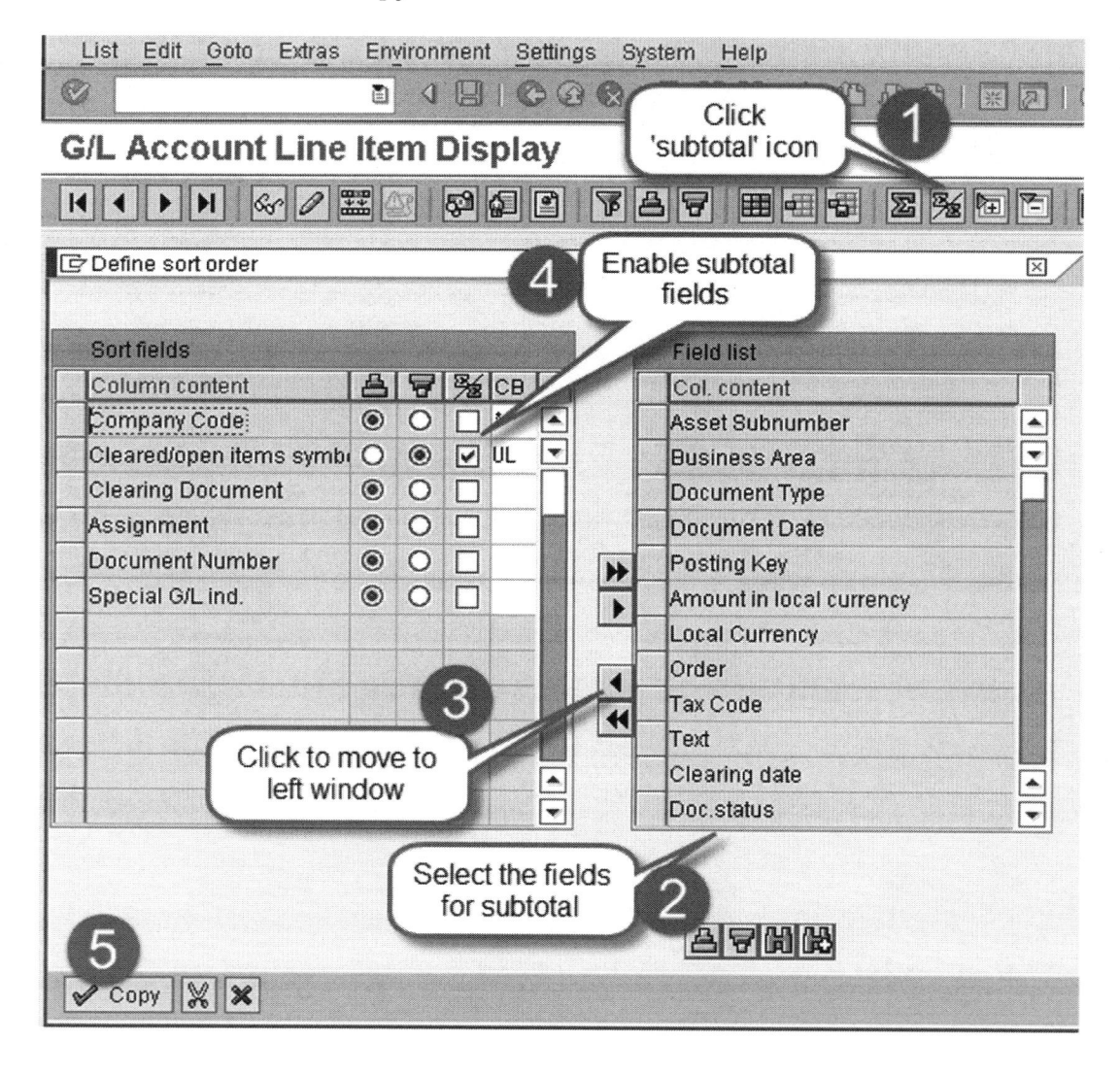

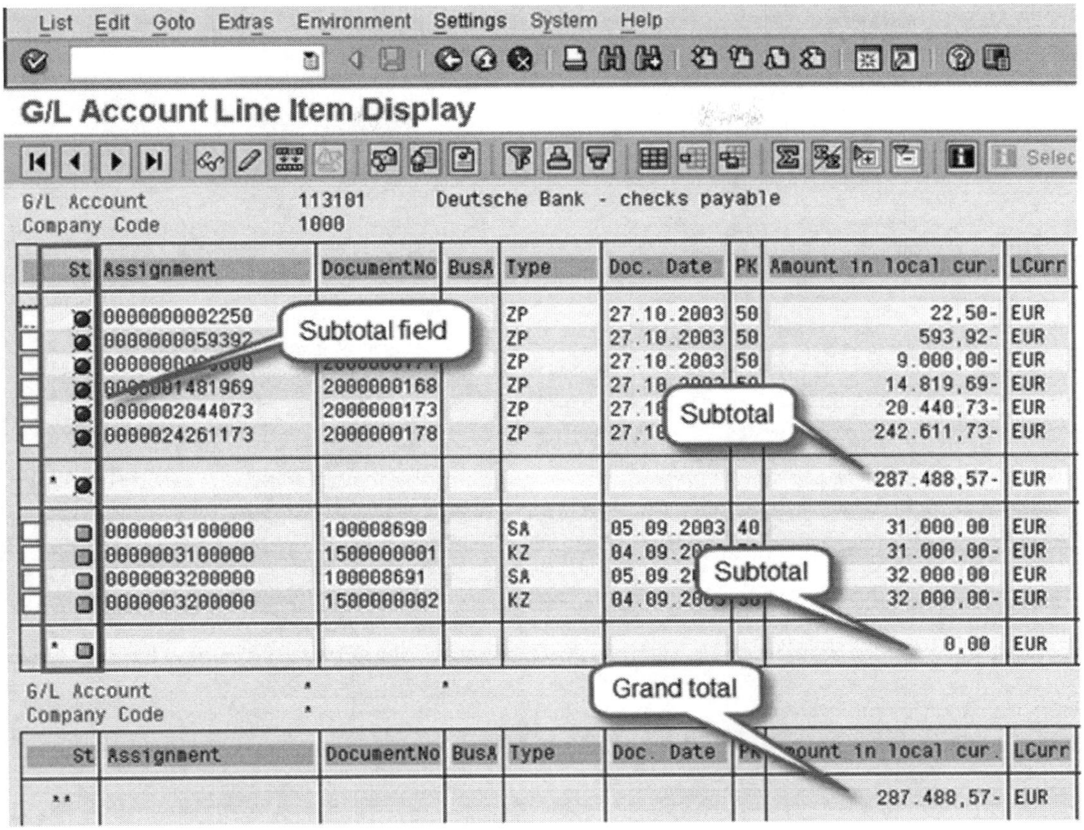

Subtotal at 'Multiple Levels'

Say First Level subtotal applied on GL account and Second Level subtotal applied on 'Cleared/Open item symbol'.

We get GL account -wise and Cleared/Open item -wise subtotals list.

106 SAP FICO BEGINNER'S HANDBOOK

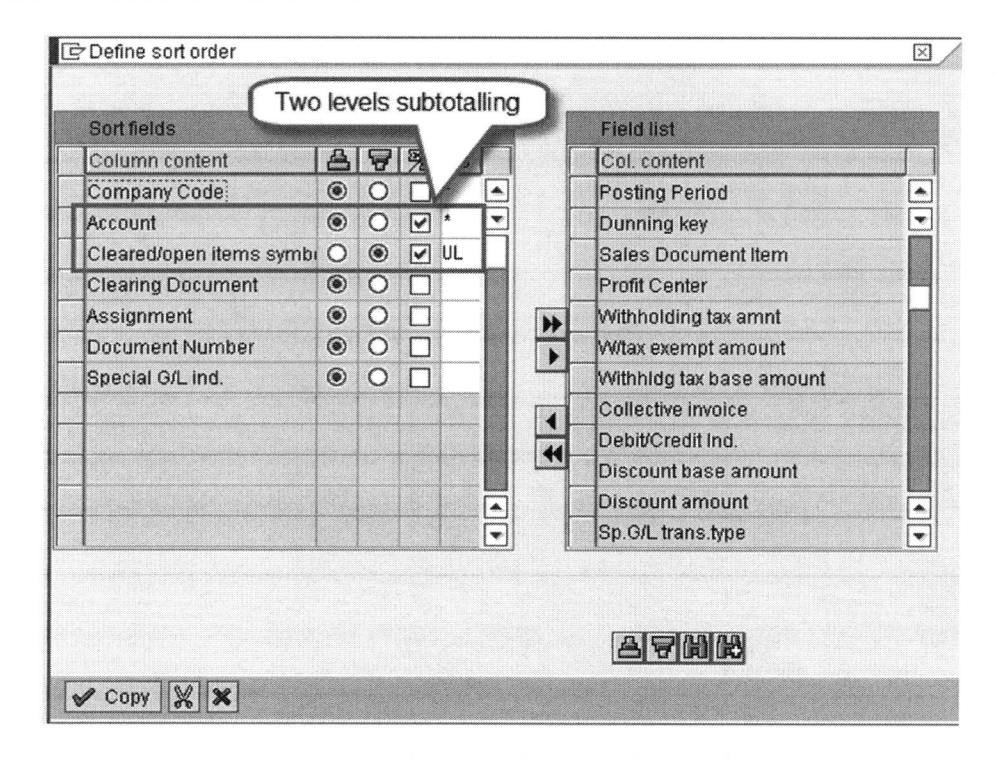

4. Know what Filter, Sort, Subtotal criteria is applied to a List

Menu path: Setting >> List Status /Ctrl+F11

List Status: Display opens to give you the snapshot view of list functions - filter, sort, subtotal applied.

Refer to the picture:

1. Calculated total records, including subtotal are 'four'.

2. Number of records above subtotal is 6 + number of records below the subtotal is 4 = 10 records.

Total records passed are 16 - Number of records filtered out is 6 = 10 records displayed.

108 SAP FICO BEGINNER'S HANDBOOK

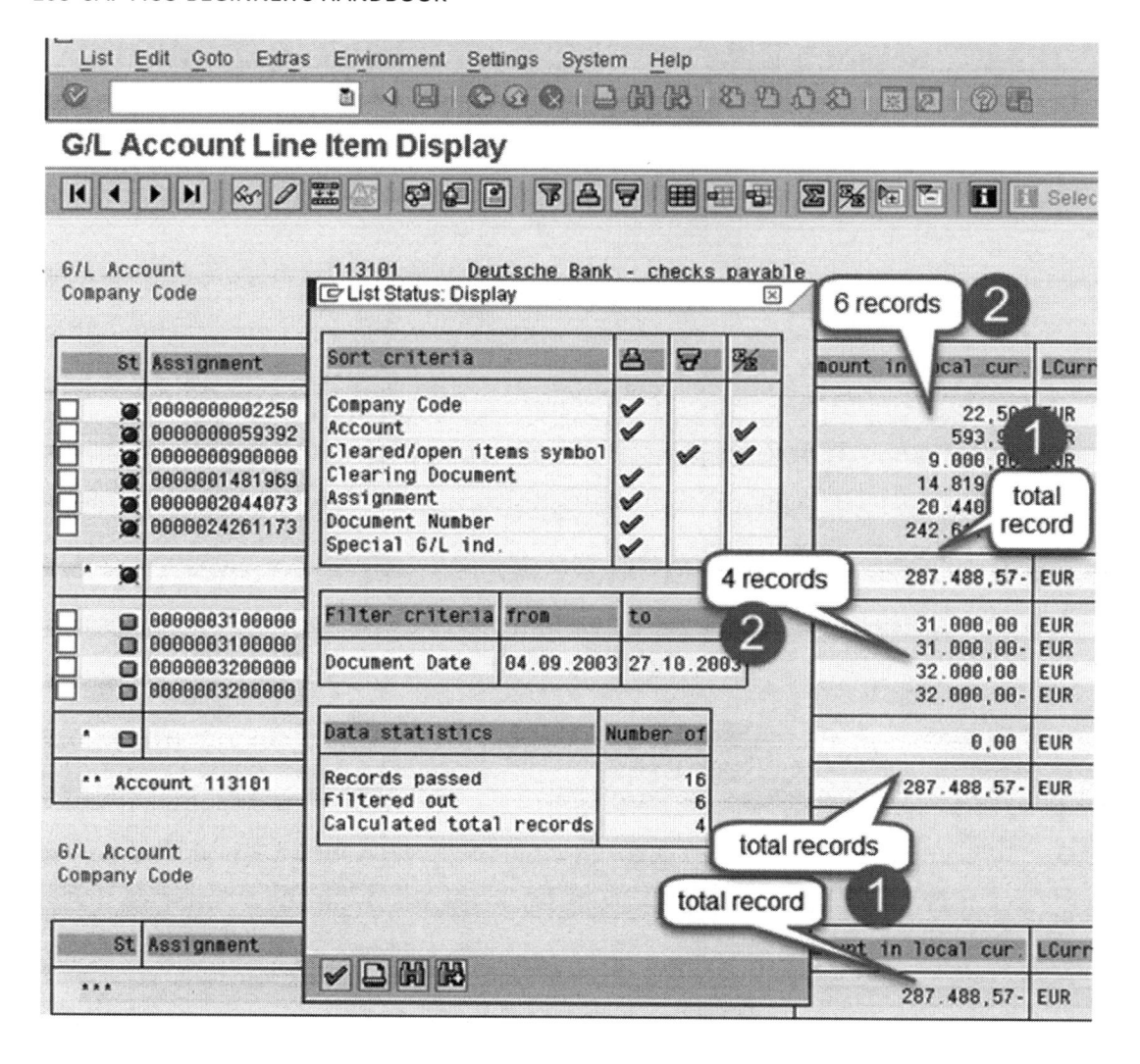

G/L Account Line Item Display

5. Display Variant

Consider you have taken time to define Filter Conditions, Sort Order, Subtotal for a List. You do not want to repeat the same exercise for every report you run during the day or every day in the morning. You can save these definitions as a DISPLAY VARIANT to be used later.

1. Menu path: Settings >> Layout >> Save, to open 'layout save as' dialogue box.

2. By default filter, sort, subtotal options are checked. You can leave it as it is to get them saved.

3. Expansion to sum level: By default, it is '0'. This means the list with this variant will display all line items.

110 SAP FICO BEGINNER'S HANDBOOK

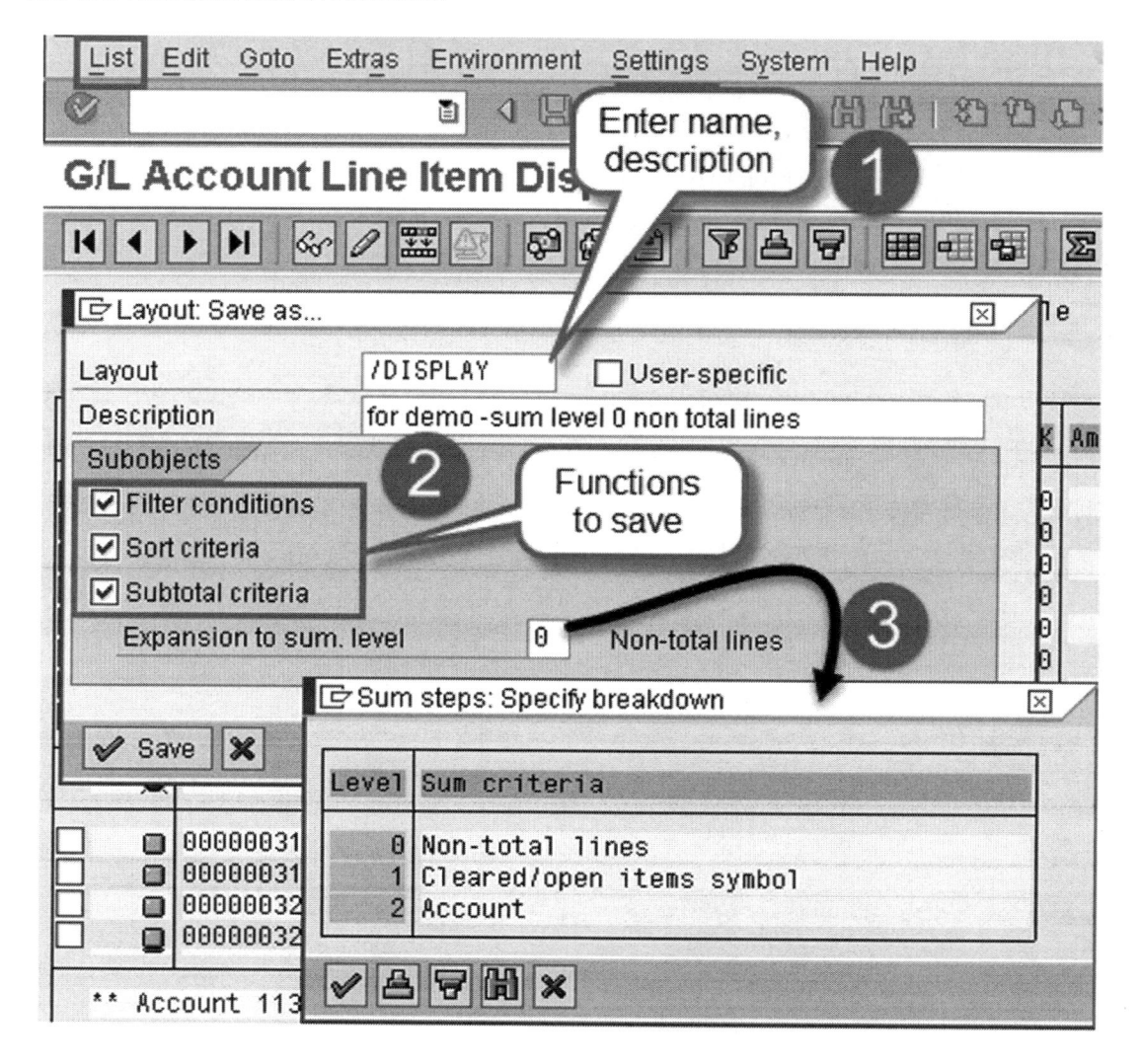

If you choose 'Expansion to sum level' as 1 or 2 as per your requirement to get the 'list' with respective summation levels.

Summation level 1 list:

Summation level 2 list:

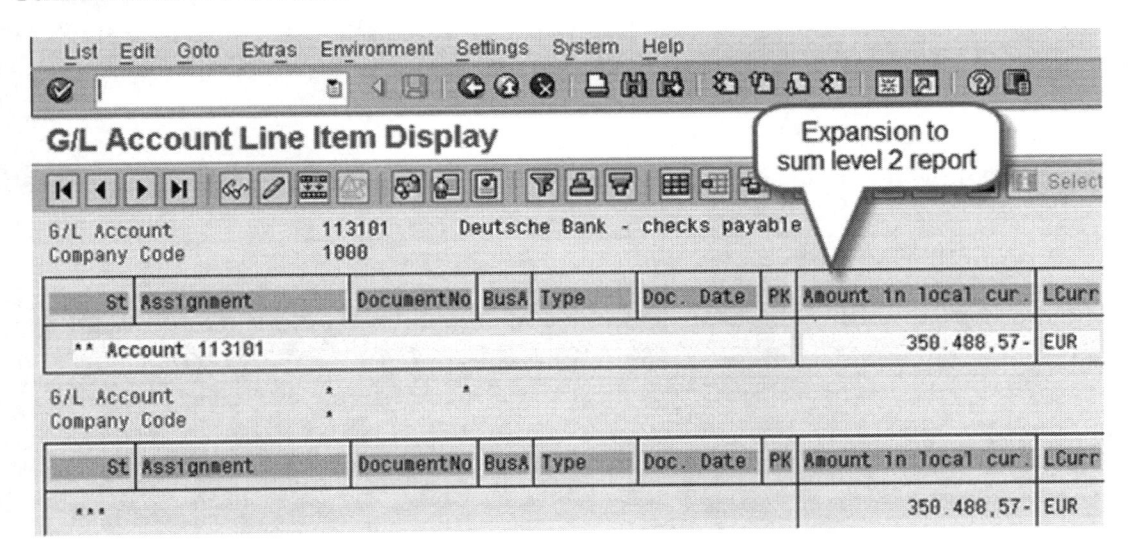

Choosing Display Variant from Selection Screen:

Ok, you have saved a Display Variant. You can use this variant in two ways to get the report you want.

112 SAP FICO BEGINNER'S HANDBOOK

1. Enter the saved 'Display variant' in <u>Selection Screen</u> under 'List output' > 'Layout field'.

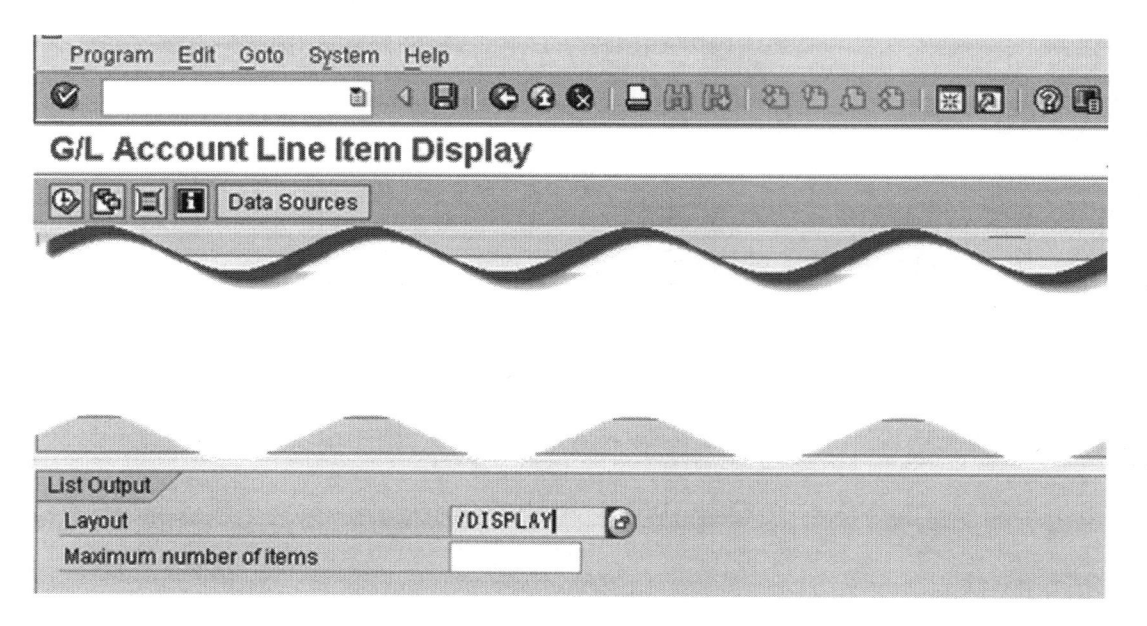

2. In case where you can't find the field for Display variant name in 'Selection Screen': You can generate the report, then follow menu path: Settings >> Layout >> Choose.

Standard Layout: **1SAP** is the standard layout that comes with the system. This cannot be modified.

To return to the Standard Layout

Say you have modified the report as per your display variant. Now you want the same report in standard format. Then follow menu path: Go to >> Basic List

∞∞

Chapter X ABC Analysis

*Experience **authority** using ABC Analysis*

∞

1. Concept of ABC Analysis

Analysis of items based on 'relative importance' is ABC analysis. As the name goes ABC Analysis, the given data is separated into three groups.

Group A, consisting of items that need highest attention of the management. Usually, Group A has smaller number of items in the whole lot. Value of each item would be high.

Group B, consisting of items that need the management attention; however, these items are of secondary importance. Usually larger in size and each item of smaller value as compared to Group A items.

Group C, consisting of least importance items; this group will have the largest in number of items and per item value the smallest as compared to Group B and Group A items.

ABC Analysis in SAP

To facilitate the demo, the list is chosen deliberately with small number of items. As the demo list has only 6 line items the concept explained above that Group C having large number of items may not be visible in the example given here under. In real world, you can apply the technique for a list having hundreds of items and you can very well see in practice the concept of ABC Analysis explained above hold good.

Important

>ABC Analysis will not work if the LIST contains both DEBIT AND CREDIT entries. The List should be either only Debit entries or Credit entries; in other words, only 'plus' or only 'minus' entries. Again, it is NOT FILTERED list of 'plus' or 'minus', but list created only of 'plus' or 'minus' from selection screen itself.

114 SAP FICO BEGINNER'S HANDBOOK

This is an enhanced function available in Lists. Please note NOT all Lists in SAP support ABC analysis.

Transaction chosen for Discussion

- TCode: FBL3N - Display/Change Line Items
- GL account 430000 Salaries, Base wages

Key Figure column: The column that contains 'amount' on which we want to do ABC Analysis.

1. Select 'Key Figure column' using mouse click.

2. <u>Menu path</u>: Go to >> ABC Analysis

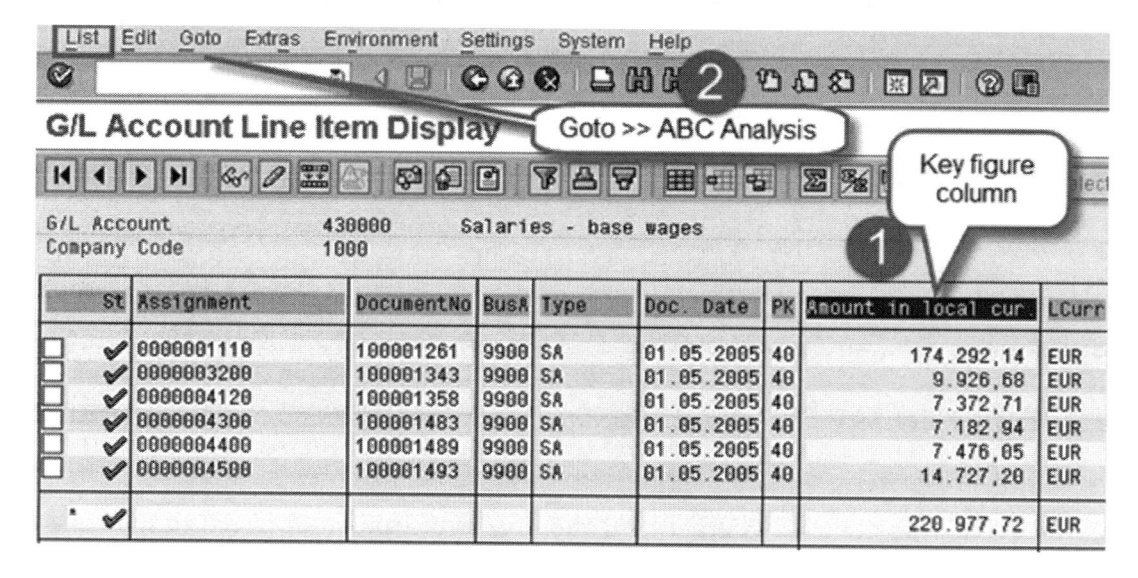

ABC Analysis can be done in

- Key Figure Percentage
- Key Figure Absolute
- Attributes Percentage

2. Key Figure Percentage Method

Step 1: Choose the first method 'KA Key Figure Percent'.

Step 2: Enter percentages for A,B,C and press 'Enter'.

Your ABC Analysis report is ready with data split into 3 groups, percentages calculated on Key Figure column.

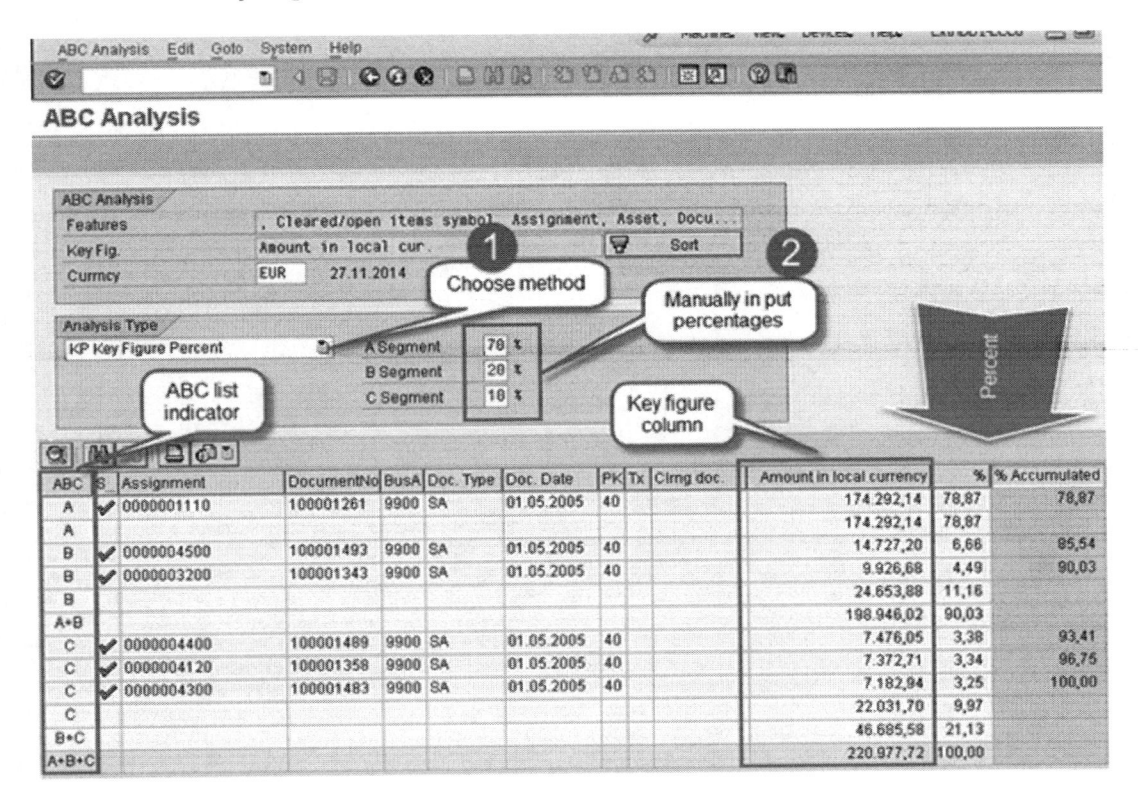

You can change the percentages, provided the total of A+B+C=100

Column Functions

ABC Analysis report has the following user-friendly column options:

- Hide Column when you don't require one
- Optimize Width, to make the report look nice
- Freeze a Column, so you can browse through columns to right of the frozen column when they go beyond the screen
- Unfreeze Column

116 SAP FICO BEGINNER'S HANDBOOK

1. Select a Column.

2. Right click to get the options.

3. Print icon to print the ABC report once you are satisfied with the column operations.

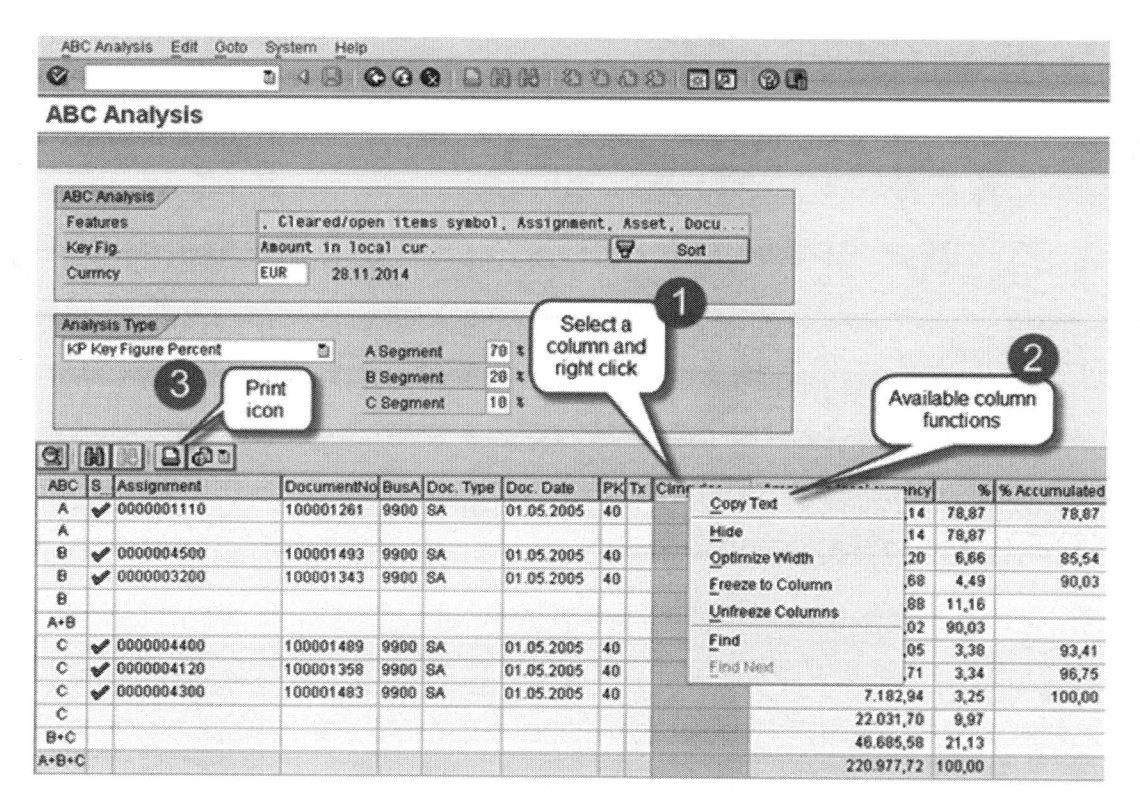

3. Key Figure Absolute Method

In this method system splits the data into three groups using Key Figure column 'Absolute' values. We need to input two values. First Value to split Group A and B and Second Value to split Group B and C.

1. Choose 'KA Key Figure Absolute' as analysis type.

2. Enter the two values and press 'Enter' to get the report.

In the picture, first split is made at 100,000. All items of value exceeding this amount will be in Group A.

Second split is made at 10,000. All items with key figure column values between 10,000 and 100,000 will be in Group B.

Rest of the items will be in Group C.

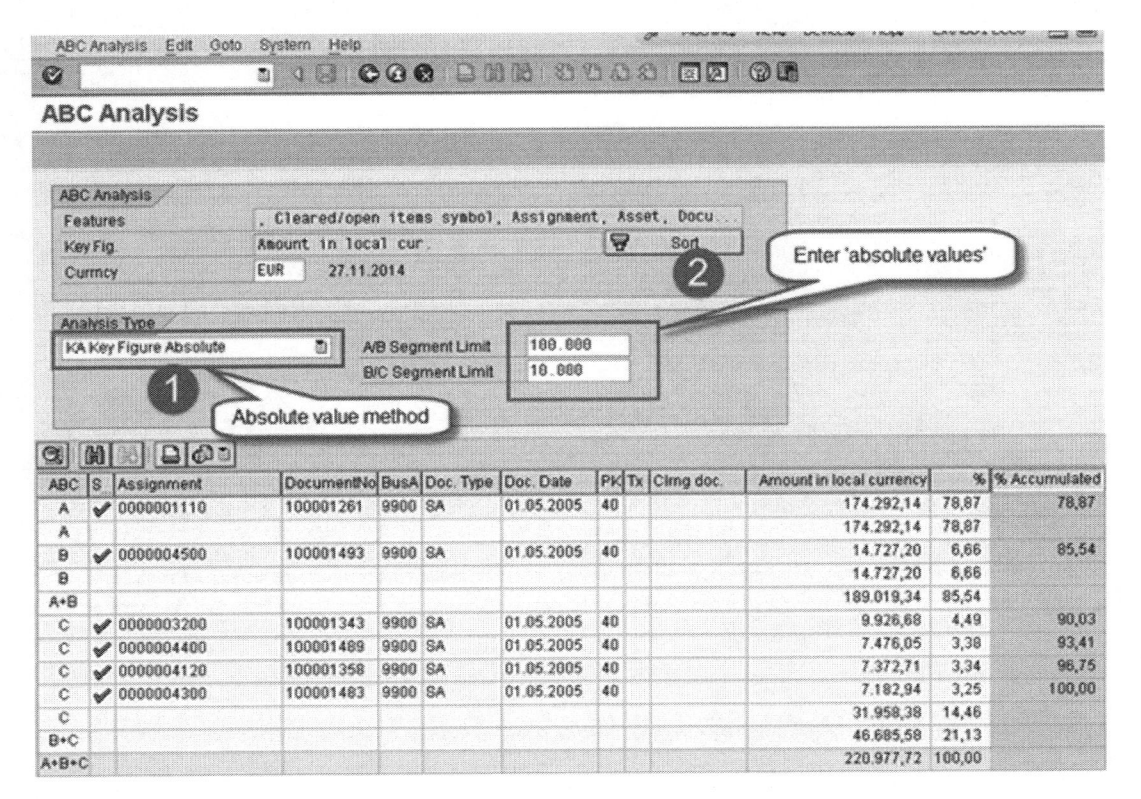

4. Attributes Percentage Method

In this analysis type number of line items in the data is considered. Percentages are calculated as **number of items to Total number of items**.

1. Choose the analysis type as 'MA Attributes Percent'.

2. Enter the percentages and press 'Enter' to get the report.

We have used 80%, 10%, 10%. Thus Group A consist of 80% in terms of number of items in the list. Similarly, Group B and C consist of 10% of total number of items.

Please note what is considered is NOT Key Figure Value for splitting but NUMBER OF ITEMS IN THE LIST.

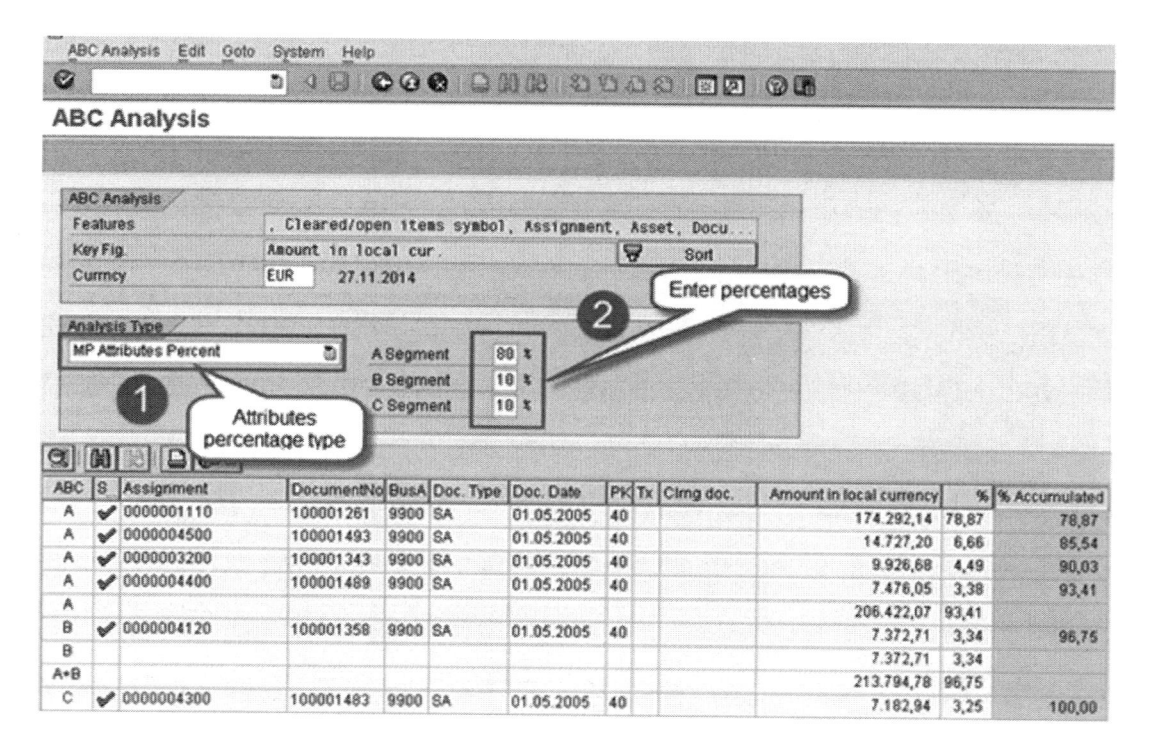

Chapter XI   Extract Management

Control YOUR report data using Extracts

∞

What is an Extract

It is a data set for a given report and selection parameters. Example you run a report for the year 20xx, period from 1 to period 16, Cost Center group H1, Cost Center Plan /Actual Comparison. The report data can be saved as an Extract.

Benefit of the saved Extract is next time when you choose to run the same report with same parameters like fiscal year, period & CC group, system prompts the Extract. If you choose to select the Extract the report is presented immediately. This is because the system does not access the data from data base tables but presents the readily available Extract.

Extract is also useful when you want to freeze the report data on a given date.

What reports Extract Management can be used?

Extract management will come in handy if you are involved in running Cost Center or Internal Order reports in 'Controlling' module - Plan /Actual comparison, Actual /Actual comparison & Target /Actual Comparison reports. Please note Target /Actual comparison reports is only for Cost Centers and this reports are not applicable for Internal Orders.

How to enable Extract

1. Menu path: Settings >> options

2. Enable 'Expert mode' in the dialogue box

3. Enable 'Create extract'

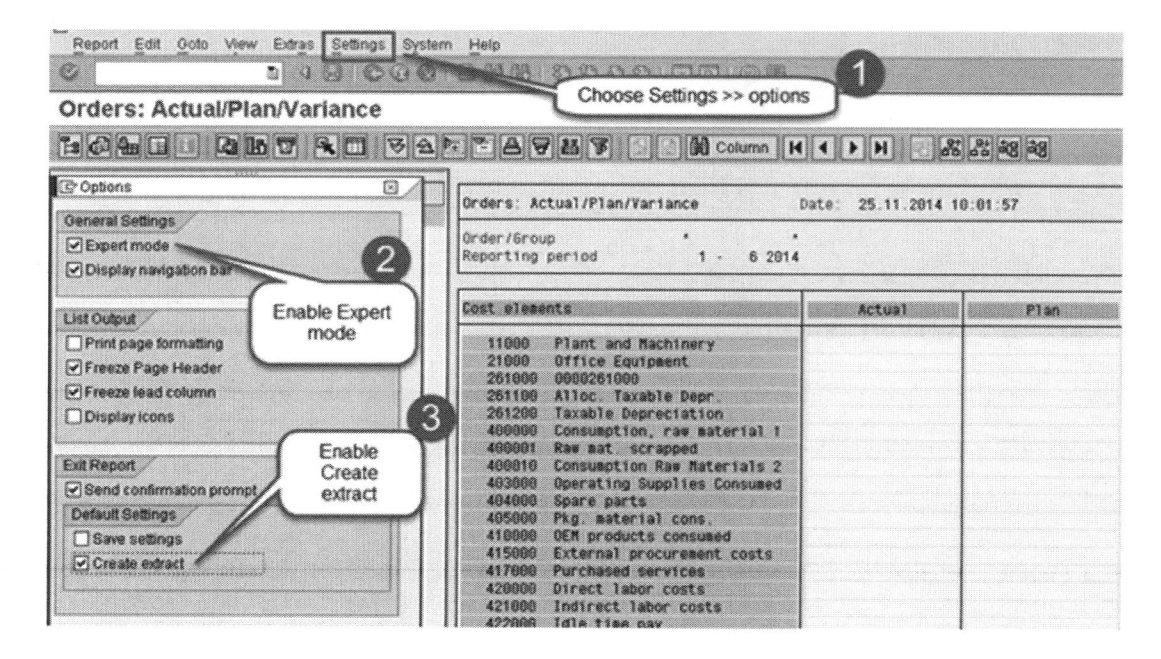

Once the above steps are completed, then whenever you exit the report, system will prompt if you want to 'Create extract'.

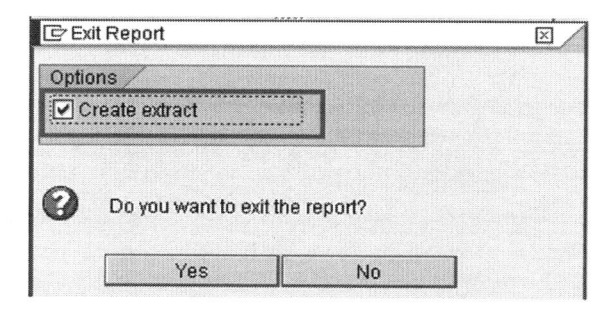

1. You can enable 'Create extract' check box if you want the report data saved for later use.

2. Give the name for the Extract.

3. Enter the number of days or the date up to which you want the data available in the system. You can also choose 'No expiration date' to keep the data in the system till you choose to delete it.

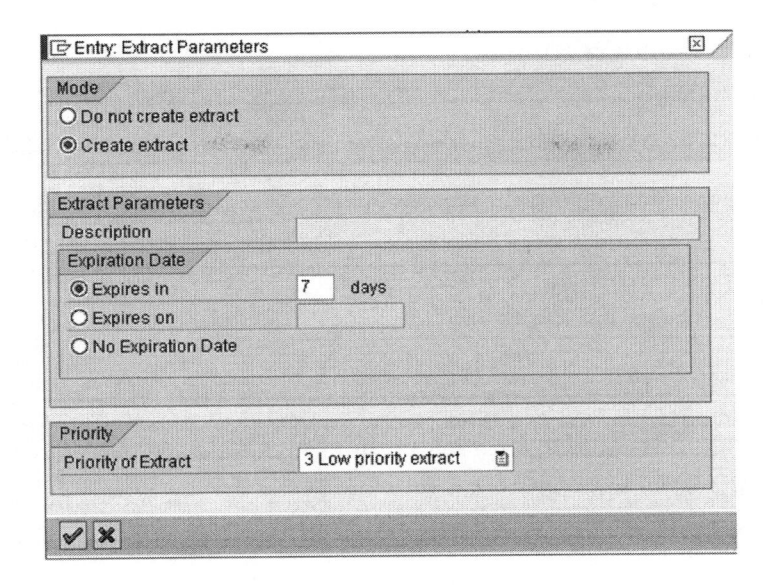

Make your choices. Extract is created and will be available as defined by you.

Refresh Option

Report >> Refresh

Consider you have a report from the Extract stored in the system. Now you want to view the report generated afresh with updated data. Use Refresh menu option under Report menu.

Naming of Extracts

Use names that can be related to the data saved as Extracts. Example -Plan Actual for May 20XX. This will be helpful when you need to get the Report from the Extract later on when the system has multiple saved Extracts.

Extract Management

Menu path: Accounting >> Controlling >> Cost Center Accounting >> Information System >> Tools

TCode: GRE0 - Extract Directory

You can get the list of extracts in the system by

- Name
- Created by

- Time of Extract Creation
- Report Group
- Priority of Extract

From the list of Extracts generated as above, you can select an Extract to:

- Change Extract Prioritization
- Change Expiry Date
- Delete

For printing the Extract list, generate the Extract list and follow menu path: Extracts >> Print Selected Extracts.

∞∞∞

A Note from the Author

Have you found this book useful? Has it delivered what it promised? In case if you are not satisfied or you have suggestions for improvement, be kind enough to send me a note at murugesan0202@yahoo.com or admin@sapficouser.com or leave your comments in https://www.facebook.com/sapficouser.

If you have enjoyed reading this book and feel benefited please, please leave your comments and ratings at Amazon page of this book. Your few words of appreciation mean so much for me!

THANKS A TON!

Good Luck and Enjoy working with SAP!

Your pal,

Murugesan Ramaswamy

Link to book's Amazon review page: http://bit.ly/amazonbookreview

For *updates on new releases & subscribing our SAP FICO USER News Letter* please visit

http://sapficouser.com

Author of this book is a Chartered Accountant and has been involved from user side under various capacities of SAP System Implementations. He can be reached at murugesan0202@yahoo.com or admin@sapficouser.com.

THANKS AGAIN FOR YOUR SUPPORT!

Made in the USA
Middletown, DE
12 August 2015